Laura Valentine

Daily communion

Laura Valentine
Daily communion
ISBN/EAN: 9783741189982
Manufactured in Europe, USA, Canada, Australia, Japa
Cover: Foto ©Lupo / pixelio.de

Manufactured and distributed by brebook publishing software (www.brebook.com)

Laura Valentine

Daily communion

BY THE SAME AUTHOR.

Uniform with this Work in size and price.

Bible Words for Daily Use

CONSISTING OF

Texts of Scripture for every Day in the Year.

    MORN: *Bible Question.*
    NOON: *Promise and Precept.*
    NIGHT: *Prayer and Praise.*

"THE book of God is a book for the heart of man; and, written *for* the heart of man, it makes *to* the heart many a direct appeal. Full and forcible are the pointed 'Questions' with which it abounds, and striking are the answers it supplies. A selection has been judged profitable for daily use.

"The work of self-examination to which such Bible-questions conduce, will serve to quicken our sense of dependence on the words of almighty 'Promise;' and every promise of God's grace should be looked upon as accompanied by an express or implied 'Precept.' When we have fitting views of dependance and of duty, we are impelled to utterances of 'Prayer;' and prayer, when answered, should give place to corresponding outbursts of 'Praise,' or to meditation on such words as may suggest and elicit a suitable feeling of thankful adoration and well-founded hope.

"Hence have arisen the threefold division and responsive arrangement of these Bible Words. The threefold division may be found an aid to the meditations of 'morning, noon, and night.'"—*See Preface.*

London : Knight & Son, Clerkenwell Close.

NEW SERIES OF
Daily Bible Text-Books.
Selected and Arranged by the
AUTHOR OF "SUNSET THOUGHTS."

Royal 64mo, on toned paper, 6d. each, cloth lettered.

1. *Daily Bible Questions.*
2. *Promises and Precepts.*
3. *Prayers and Praises.*
4. *Morning Vows.*
5. *Noontide Helps.*
6. *Evening Voices.*

Note.—Nos. 1–3 may be had in one volume, under the title "BIBLE WORDS FOR DAILY USE." Small Edition, 1s. 6d. larger Edition, IN TWO COLOURS, 2s. 6d., bevelled boards, extra cloth, gilt. Nos. 4–6, also in one volume, uniform in size and price, under the title of "DAILY COMMUNION."

BY THE SAME AUTHOR.

1. Our Home Above; or, Echoes from Canaan.
2. Watchwords for the Happy.
3. Whispers to the Sick and Sorrowing.
4. Come and See; or, Words for the Doubter.
5. Look and Live; or, Words for the Inquirer.
6. Up and be Doing; or, Words for the Christian.

The above Six, uniform with the "Bible Text-Books," are preparing for publication. No. 1 will be shortly ready.

London: Knight & Son, Clerkenwell Close.

DAILY COMMUNION.

CONSISTING OF

1.—MORNING VOWS.
2.—NOONTIDE HELPS.
3.—EVENING VOICES.

𝔖𝔢𝔩𝔢𝔠𝔱𝔢𝔡 𝔞𝔫𝔡 𝔄𝔯𝔯𝔞𝔫𔤤𔢢𔡡
BY THE AUTHOR OF
"BIBLE WORDS FOR DAILY USE;"
"Sunset Thoughts," etc.

LONDON: KNIGHT & SON,
12, CLERKENWELL CLOSE.

PREFACE.

IT is a seemly thing that our morning prayers should be accompanied by "Morning Vows." It is a mockery to ask for guidance and help, unless we are prepared to yield obedience and submission. The most eminent saints of all ages have been those, who, like Joshua, and David, and Paul, have been men of earnest decision and dauntless purpose. Their words of holy vow let us adopt. A selection has been prepared for daily use. It will be seen that the greater number are vows of praise. This is simply a Scriptural proportion. In our vows, we are too often self-seeking. With the glory of God more steadfastly in view, our own holiness would be more rapidly advanced.

If we would have the vows of morning kept, we need to lift up a midday barrier against the

Preface.

inroads of worldliness. It is but a fleeting moment that the masses among us can command. Yet that moment might be turned to profit, and for this purpose "Noontide Helps" may be welcome. A text and a verse, speedily but thoughtfully read, may no less speedily work a stimulating and strengthening effect.

The "Evening Voices" which follow are intended as a guide to the evening duty of self-examination,—a duty which, it is to be feared, many neglect, because some pervert, —a duty, nevertheless, which may bring with it a daily blessing, by deepening our penitence, quickening our zeal, and giving definiteness to our prayers and praises.

May the God of Bethel, the God of Zion, the God who in public and in private draws near to His people with a blessing, grant us to know more and more the privilege of "Daily Communion" with Himself.

Daily Communion.

JANUARY 1.

Morning:—

"This will we do, if God permit."
—*Heb.* vi. 3.
Our hearts shall beat for Thee alone;
Our lives shall make Thy goodness known.

Noon:—

"The Lord...guided them on every side."—2 *Chron.* xxxii. 22.
Whate'er the path these mortal feet may trace,
Breathe through my soul the blessings of Thy grace.

Evening:—

Have I sought—and have I found—
a New Year's blessing from on high?
—(*Numb.* vi. 24—26.)
The night is come, the hour for peaceful rest;
O Saviour, bless us,—then we must be blest.

JANUARY 2.

MORNING :—

"We will bless the Lord from this time forth, and for evermore."— *Psa.* cxv. 18.

'Tis His to number out our days;
'Tis ours to spend them for His praise.

NOON :—

"He led them forth by the right way, that they might go to a city of habitation: oh, that men would praise the Lord for His goodness."—*Psa.* cvii. 7, 8.

My soul with pleasure shall obey,
And follow where He leads the way.

EVENING :—

Have I taken God for the Guide of my life?—(*Psa.* lxxiii. 24.)

Then bravely I can meet each day,
And fear it not, come what come may.
My heart grows strong; all fear must fly,
When once I feel Thy love, Most High!

JANUARY 3.

MORNING :—

"We will remember Thy love."—
S. Song i. 4.

 Should sorrows high o'er sorrows swell,
 Let mercy smile, and all is well.

NOON :—

"He led them on safely, so that they feared not."—*Psa.* lxxviii. 53.

 Captain of Israel's host, and Guide
  Of all who seek the land above,
 Beneath Thy shadow we abide,
  The cloud of Thy protecting love;
 *   *   *   *
 As safe from danger as from fear,
 While love, almighty love, is near.

EVENING :—

Has God the chief place in my affections?—(*Psa.* lxxiii. 25.)

Let me enjoy but Thee, I crave no better lot;
For, having Thee alone, what have I not?
I wish not sea or land, nor would I be [Thee.
Of heaven possess'd, heaven unpossess'd of

JANUARY 4.

MORNING :—

"In the morning shall my prayer prevent Thee."—*Psa*. lxxxviii. 13.

Now let the glory of Thy dawning
　On our benighted souls arise ;
Where'er Thou shinest, Star of morning,
　The gloom of sin and sorrow flies.

NOON :—

"Daniel kneeled upon his knees three times a day, and prayed, and gave thanks."—*Dan*. vi. 10.

When noon her throne in light arrays,
　To Thee my soul in triumph springs,
Thee, throned in glory's endless blaze,
　Thee, Lord of lords, and King of kings.

EVENING :—

What is my errand to the mercy-seat to night ?—(*Matt*. xx. 32.)

Abide with me ; fast falls the eventide ;
The darkness thickens ; Lord, with me abide ;
While other helpers fail and comforts flee,
Help of the helpless, oh ! abide with me.

JANUARY 5.

Morning:—

"Evening, and morning, and at noon, will I pray."—*Psa.* lv. 17.

> He guides our feet, He guards our way,
> His morning smiles bless all the day;
> He spreads the evening veil, and keeps
> The silent hours while Israel sleeps.

Noon:—

"The Lord shall be thy confidence."—*Prov.* iii. 26.

> His presence shall my wants supply,
> And guard me with a watchful eye;
> My noonday walks He will attend,
> And all my midnight hours defend.

Evening:—

Is this evening such as I would wish life's evening to be?—(*Zech.* xiv. 7.)

> Thy light upon our evening pour;
> Oh, may our souls no sunset see,
> But death to us an open door
> To an eternal morning be.

JANUARY 6.

MORNING :—

"In the night His song shall be with me, and my prayer unto the God of my life."—*Psa.* xlii. 8.

> Thou Giver of songs in the night,
>   Of joy in the deepest distress,
> I sigh to be fill'd with Thy light,
>   I long for a glimpse of Thy face.

NOON :—

"We have a great High Priest."—*Heb.* iv. 14 (*comp.* 15).

> Thou who didst sit on Jacob's well
>   At weary hour of noon,
> The languid pulses Thou canst tell,
>   The nerveless spirit tune.

EVENING :—

Do my hopes of heaven grow daily brighter?—(*Rom.* viii. 25.)

> A few more suns shall set
>   O'er these dark hills of time,
> And we shall be where suns are not;—
>   A far serener clime!

JANUARY 7.

MORNING:—

"The Lord our God...preserved us;...therefore will we also serve the Lord."—*Josh.* xxiv. 17, 18.

> Let every thought, and work, and word,
>   To Thee be ever given;
> Then life shall be Thy service, Lord,
>   And death the gate of heaven.

NOON:—

"There shall be a reward."—*Prov.* xxiv. 14.

> Rest, rest from anxious thought!
>   From pressing, hurrying care!
> Rest *here* so vainly sought,
>   So richly furnish'd *there*!

EVENING:—

How can I get my faith strengthened?—(*Rom.* xv. 13.)

> Let Thy love shine upon my soul, and chase
>   This mistiness and darkness quite away,
> Till Faith discerns her holy resting-place
>   Distinctly in the perfect light of day.

JANUARY 8.

MORNING :—

"We will go into His tabernacles; we will worship at His footstool."—*Psa.* cxxxii. 7.

> With early feet I love to appear
> Among Thy saints, and seek Thy face;
> Oft have I seen Thy glory there,
> And felt the power of sovereign grace.

NOON :—

"His favour is as dew upon the grass."—*Prov.* xix. 12.

> The dew lies thick on all the ground,
> Shall my poor fleece be dry?
> The manna rains from heaven around,
> Shall I of hunger die?

EVENING :—

Where do I get my griefs soothed?—(*Heb.* iv. 16.)

> There is a heavenly mercy-seat
> To calm the sinner's fears;
> There is a Saviour at whose feet
> The mourner dries his tears.

JANUARY 9.

MORNING :—

"We will rejoice in Thy salvation, and in the name of our God we will set up our banners."—*Psa.* xx. 5.

    Faint not, Christian, though the world
    Has its hostile flag unfurl'd ;
    Hold the cross of Jesus fast,
    Thou shalt overcome at last.

NOON :—

"He preserveth the way of His saints."—*Prov.* ii. 8.

    Oh, guide our doubtful feet aright,
      And keep us in Thy ways;
    And while we turn our vows to prayers,
      Turn Thou our prayers to praise.

EVENING :—

Why have I left so many vows unfulfilled?—(*Prov.* xxviii. 26.)

    I was too bold; he never yet stood sure
      That stands secure !
    Who ever trusted to his native strength
      But fell at length ?

JANUARY 10.

MORNING :—

"I will walk before the Lord in the land of the living."—*Psa.* cxvi. 9.

> A pilgrim here I wander,
>   On earth have no abode;
> My father-land is yonder,
>   My home is with my God.

NOON :—

"The wise shall inherit glory."—*Prov.* iii. 35.

> My spirit seeks its dwelling yonder;
>   And faith foredates the joyful day,
> When yon blue skies shall cease to sunder
>   The one dear love-link'd family.

EVENING :—

What seed have I this day been sowing?—(*Rev.* xiv. 14—19.)

> Eternity is but Time's harvest-home;
> Futurity the blossom of To-day;
> What thou dost sow, in measure and in kind,
> That also shalt thou reap.

JANUARY 11.

Morning:—

"I will never forget Thy precepts; for with them Thou hast quickened me."—*Psa.* cxix. 93.

> Let sacred duties every day
> Our highest pleasure be;
> And, in Thine own appointed way,
> Conduct our souls to Thee.

Noon:—

"My son, be wise, and make my heart glad."—*Prov.* xxvii. 11.

> Ask for light to know God's will,
> Ask for love thy heart to fill,
> Ask for faith to bear thee on
> Through the might of Christ His Son.

Evening:—

How have I discharged this day's duties?—(*Matt.* xi. 29.)

Oh, take My yoke,—the blest Redeemer cries,
Divine compassion beaming in His eyes,—
Learn thou of Me; My teaching shall impart
Truth to thy mind, and comfort to thy heart.

JANUARY 12.

MORNING:—

"So shall I keep Thy law continually for ever and ever."—*Psa.* cxix. 44.

High Heaven, that heard the solemn vow,
   That vow renew'd shall daily hear,
Till in life's latest hour I bow,
   And bless in death a bond so dear.

NOON:—

"The light of the righteous rejoiceth."—*Prov.* xiii. 9.

When black the threatening clouds appear,
   And storms my path invade,
That voice shall tranquillize each fear,
   "'Tis I, be not afraid."

EVENING:—

How have I accepted this day's privations?—(*Job* i. 21.)

   Ne'er murmur at His high decrees,
     Who gives and takes away;
   But, grateful for His mercies past,
     Prize those He gives to-day.

JANUARY 13.

Morning:—

"I will wait on Thy name; for it is good before Thy saints."—*Psa.* lii. 9.

> There is a name I love to hear;
> I love to speak its worth:
> It sounds like music in my ear,
> The sweetest name on earth.

Noon:—

"He that waiteth on his Master shall be honoured."—*Prov.* xxvii. 18.

> Does the way seem long and drear
> To thy sad bewilder'd sight?
> Pray; and thou wilt see Him near;
> Wait; He'll lead thee to the light.

Evening:—

Do I wait in hopeful faith, or idle unbelief?—(*Luke* xii. 35, 36.)

> Pilgrim, weeping at the gate,
> Hear His message,...pray and wait!
> Seek Him early, seek Him late;
> Fear not, doubt not;—pray AND wait!

JANUARY 14.

MORNING:—

"I will lift up my hands in Thy name."—*Psa.* lxiii. 4.

> Thou ever good and kind!
> A thousand reasons move,
> A thousand obligations bind,
> My heart to grateful love.

NOON:—

"The eyes of the Lord are in every place, beholding the evil and the good."—*Prov.* xv. 3.

> He knows our souls in all their fears,
> And gently wipes our falling tears,
> Forms trembling voices to a song,
> And bids the feeble heart be strong.

EVENING:—

Do I add praying to working?—(*Matt.* xxvi. 41.)

> Our oars alone can ne'er prevail
> To reach the distant coast;
> The breath of heaven must swell the sail,
> Or all the toil is lost.

JANUARY 15.

Morning :—

"I will glorify Thy name for evermore."—*Psa.* lxxxvi. 12.

> O Lord, how excellent Thy name!
> How manifold Thy ways!
> Let time Thy saving truth proclaim;
> Eternity, Thy praise.

Noon :—

"The path of the just is as the shining light, that shineth more and more unto the perfect day."—*Prov.* iv. 18.

> In paths unknown He leads them on
> To His divine abode,
> And shows new miracles of grace
> Through all the heavenly road.

Evening :—

Do I exercise the patience of hope?—(*Rom.* xii. 12.)

> What if thou always suffer tribulation,
> And if thy Christian warfare never cease?
> The gaining of the quiet habitation
> Shall gather thee to everlasting peace.

JANUARY 16.

MORNING:—

"As thou livest, and as thy soul liveth, I will not do this thing."— 2 *Sam.* xi. 11.

No! let a careless world repose,
   And slumber on through life's short day,
While Israel to the conflict goes,
   And bears the glorious prize away.

NOON:—

"Even Christ pleased not Himself." —*Rom.* xv. 3.

Be Thou my pattern; make me bear
More of Thy gracious image here;
Then God the Judge shall own my name
Amongst the followers of the Lamb.

EVENING:—

Am I selfishly careful of my own ease?—(*Rom.* xv. 1, 2.)

Let love through all my conduct shine,
An image fair, though faint of Thine;
Let me Thine humble follower prove,
Father of grace, and God of love.

JANUARY 17.

Morning:—

"I will keep my mouth with a bridle, while the wicked is before me."—*Psa.* xxxix. 1.

 Spirit of grace, all meek and mild,
  Inspire our breasts, our souls possess;
 Repel each passion rude and wild,
  And bless us as we aim to bless.

Noon:—

"When He suffered, He threatened not."—1 *Pet.* ii. 23.

 For ever on Thy burden'd heart
  A weight of sorrow hung,
 Yet no ungentle, murmuring word
  Escaped Thy silent tongue.

Evening:—

Do I strive after conformity to Christ?—(*Rom.* viii. 29.)

 Thy fair example may we trace,
  To teach us what we ought to be;
 Make us, by Thy transforming grace,
  Dear Saviour, daily more like Thee.

JANUARY 18.

MORNING :—

"My heart shall not reproach me so long as I live."—*Job* xxvii. 6.

    Happy the meek, whose gentle breast,
        Clear as the summer's evening ray,
    Calm as the regions of the blest,
        Enjoys on earth celestial day.

NOON :—

"Let us run with patience the race that is set before us, looking unto Jesus."—*Heb.* xii. 1, 2.

    Looking off unto Jesus,
        My spirit is blest ;
    In the world I have turmoil,
        In Him I have rest.

EVENING :—

Have I been sprinkled from an evil conscience ?—(*Heb.* x. 22.)

    Here at Thy cross I still would wait,
        Nor from its shelter flee,
    Till Thou, O God, in mercy great,
        Art merciful to me.

JANUARY 19.

MORNING :—

"I will declare mine iniquity; I will be sorry for my sin."—*Psa.* xxxviii. 18.

> Lord, my heart is bare before Thee,
> Let me now Thy mercy prove:
> Help me, for my wants implore Thee;
> Love me with a Father's love.

NOON :—

"The chastisement of our peace was upon Him."—*Isa.* liii. 5.

> Before the cross of Him who died,
> Behold I prostrate fall:
> Let every sin be crucified,
> And Christ be all in all.

EVENING :—

Have I truly repented of sin?—(*Zech.* xii. 10.)

> Mourning, I see my lost estate;
> Yet dare in faith to cry,
> Oh! let my evil nature die,
> Another heart in me create.

JANUARY 20.

MORNING :—

"I will bear the indignation of the Lord, because I have sinned against Him."—*Mic.* vii. 9.

>Why is it thus? why hope we yet
> To outlive each blast of ill?
>One—One—for us the storm hath met,
> His aid is with us still.

NOON :—

"A wounded spirit who can bear?" —*Prov.* xviii. 14.

>Oh, may we hear Thy gracious word
> Pronounce our sorrows past;
>Establish Thou our goings, Lord,
> While these our wanderings last.

EVENING :—

Have I beheld the Lamb of God? (*John* i. 29.)

>Guilty I plead before Thy throne;
> O God, my crimes forgive;
>I plead the Saviour's blood alone;
> Pardon, and bid me live.

JANUARY 21.

Morning :—

"I will make mention of Thy righteousness, even of Thine only."—*Psa.* lxxi. 16.

To Thee, Thou bleeding Lamb, to Thee,
For pardon, peace, and life, we flee;
The shelter of Thy cross we claim;
Thy righteousness alone we name.

Noon :—

"Ye shall abide in Him."—1 *John* ii. 27.

Oh, abide, abide in Jesus,
  Who Himself for ever lives;
Who from death eternal frees us;
  Yea, who life eternal gives.

Evening :—

Am I walking as Christ walked?— (1 *John* ii. 6.)

Ye who the name of Jesus bear,
  His sacred steps pursue;
And let that mind which was in Him
  Be also found in you.

JANUARY 22.

MORNING :—

"I will fetch my knowledge from afar."—*Job* xxxvi. 3.

  Blest Saviour, though my knowledge reach
  To all that human systems teach,
  How small the learning I possess,
  If all unknown Thy righteousness!

NOON :—

"Now I know in part; but then shall I know even as also I am known."—1 *Cor.* xiii. 12.

  Oh, argument for truth divine,
    For study's cares, for virtue's strife,
  To know the enjoyment will be thine
    In that reserved, that endless life!

EVENING :—

"Have I learned the first elements of true wisdom?—(*Psa.* cxi. 10.)

  Bless'd are the souls that hear and know
    The gospel's joyful sound;
  Peace shall attend the path they go,
    And light their steps surround.

JANUARY 23.

MORNING :—

"I will consider Thy testimonies."
—*Psa.* cxix. 95.

I'll read the histories of Thy love,
  And keep Thy laws in sight,
While through the promises I rove
  With ever fresh delight.

NOON :—

"Blessed are they that dwell in Thy house; they will be still praising Thee."—*Psa.* lxxxiv. 4.

Lord, 'tis a pleasant thing to stand
In gardens planted by Thy hand;
Let me within Thy courts be seen,
Like a young cedar, fresh and green.

EVENING :—

Can my soul prosper without aid from above?—(*Isa.* xxxv. 1.)

I want the grace that springs from Thee,
  That quickens all things where it flows,
And makes a wretched thorn like me
  Bloom as the myrtle or the rose.

JANUARY 24.

MORNING :—

"I have said that I would keep Thy words."—*Psa.* cxix. 57.

> Prone as we are from Thee to stray,
> Our only Strength and Guide,
> Oh, lead us in Thy righteous way,
> Nor let our footsteps slide.

NOON :—

"As a bird that wandereth from her nest, so is a man that wandereth from his place."—*Prov.* xxvii. 8.

> How foolish thus from love and peace,
> So raven-like, to roam!
> Lord, let my wretched wanderings cease,
> And, dove-like, lead me home.

EVENING :—

Do I hate or encourage wandering thoughts ?—(*Jer.* xiv. 10.)

> Far from my thoughts, vain world, begone!
> Let my religious hours alone;
> Fain would my eyes my Saviour see,
> I wait a visit, Lord, from Thee.

JANUARY 25.

Morning :—

"I will sing of Thy POWER."—*Psa.* lix. 16.

> Oh, when His wisdom can mistake,
> His might decay, His love forsake,
> Then may His children cease to sing,
> The Lord Omnipotent is King.

Noon :—

"A crown was given unto Him; and He went forth, conquering and to conquer."—*Rev.* vi. 2.

> Wide Thy resistless sceptre sway,
> Till all Thine enemies obey!
> Wide may Thy cross its virtues prove,
> And conquer millions by its love!

Evening :—

Do I look to God as a Strength-Giver?—(*Psa.* xxix. 11.)

> The Lord shall give His people strength,
>   And bid their sorrows cease;
> The Lord shall bless His chosen race
>   With everlasting peace.

JANUARY 26.

MORNING :—

"Yea, I will sing aloud of Thy MERCY in the morning."—*Psa.* lix. 16.

New time, new favours, and new joys,
   Do a new song require;
Till we shall praise Thee as we would,
   Accept our heart's desire.

NOON :—

"Having loved His own which were in the world, He loved them unto the end."—*John* xiii. 1.

How sweet to think in sorrow's hour
   That He who reigns above,
Although supreme in sovereign power,
   Is as supreme in love.

EVENING :—

Have the stars of night a voice for me?—(*Job* xxv. 5, 6.)

They tell not only of the might
   Of Him enthroned above,
But trace in characters of light
   His mercy and His love.

JANUARY 27.

Morning:—

"I will also praise Thee with the psaltery, even Thy TRUTH, O my God."—*Psa.* lxxi. 22.

> Cast thy burden on the Lord,
> Plead His promise, trust His word,
> So shalt thou have cause to bless
> His eternal faithfulness.

Noon:—

"He...was called Faithful and True."
—*Rev.* xix. 11.

> On Jesu's plighted love,
> In every state rely;
> The very hidings of His face
> Shall train thee up for joy.

Evening:—

Am I a faithful follower of the faithful Saviour?—(*Rev.* xvii. 14.)

> Leader of faithful souls, and Guide
> Of all who travel to the sky,
> Come, and with us, even us, abide,
> Who would on Thee alone rely.

JANUARY 28.

Morning:

"As for me, I will call upon God; and the Lord shall save me."—*Psa.* lv. 16.

> Though rocks and quicksands deep
> Through all my passage lie,
> Yet Christ will safely keep,
> And guide me with His eye.

Noon:

"Some...concerning faith have made shipwreck."—1 *Tim.* i. 19.

Touch Thou my compass, and renew my sails;
Send stiffer courage, or send milder gales;
New-cast my plummet; make it apt to try
Where the rocks lurk, and where the quick-
                              [sands lie.

Evening:—

Have I a safeguard amid life's storms?—(*Heb.* vi. 19.)

> How oft, when tempest-toss'd at night,
> I watch in vain for dawning light,—
> Yet think, when terrors would prevail,
> My anchor is within the veil.

JANUARY 29.

Morning:—

"Unto God would I commit my cause."—*Job* v. 8.

The sun and every vassal-star,
All space, beyond the soar of angel-wings,
 Wait on His word; and yet He stays His car,
For every sigh a contrite suppliant brings.

Noon:—

"Be not afraid of sudden fear, neither of the desolation of the wicked."—*Prov.* iii. 25.

He comes with succour speedy
 To those who suffer wrong;
To help the poor and needy,
 And bid the weak be strong.

Evening:—

Are mine the prayers of a penitent?
—(*Psa.* li. 1—3.)

O hear my supplication,
 For I am poor and weak;
Hear, hear with acceptation,
 The tear-dew'd words I speak.

JANUARY 30.

MORNING:—

"I will pray with the spirit, and I will pray with the understanding also."—1 *Cor.* xiv. 15.

Lord, when we bend before Thy throne,
　And our confessions pour,
Teach us to feel the sins we own,
　And hate what we deplore.

NOON:—

"While they are yet speaking, I will hear."—*Isa.* lxv. 24.

Oh, there is never a sorrow of heart
　That shall lack a timely end,
If but to God we turn, and ask
　Of Him to be our Friend.

EVENING:—

Do I seek holiness as well as happiness?—(*Heb.* xii. 14.)

O Lord, I look to Thee,
　To Thee lift up my heart;
In heaven I would Thy glory see,—
　Now, therefore, grace impart.

JANUARY 31.

MORNING :—

"God hath spoken in His holiness; I will rejoice."—*Psa.* lx. 6.

Ye mourning pilgrims, cease your tears,
  And hush each sigh of sorrow;
The light of that bright morn appears,
  The long Sabbatic morrow.

NOON :—

"The poor among men shall rejoice in the Holy One of Israel."—*Isa.* xxix. 19.

God is the treasure of my soul,
  The source of lasting joy,
A joy which want shall not impair,
  Nor death itself destroy.

EVENING :—

Do I know in whom I have believed?—(2 *Tim.* i. 12.)

My spirit on thy care,
  Blest Saviour, I recline;
Thou wilt not leave me in despair,
  For Thou art Love Divine.

FEBRUARY 1.

MORNING:—
"I will be glad in the Lord."—
Psa. civ. 34.

If loving hearts were never lonely,—
If all they like might always be,—
Accepting what they wish for only,
They might be glad,—but not in Thee.

NOON:—
"He hath commanded His covenant for ever."—*Psa.* cxi. 9.

Engraved as in eternal brass
The mighty promise shines;
Nor can the powers of darkness rase
Those everlasting lines.

EVENING:—
Have I joy in the midst of sorrow?
—(2 *Cor.* viii. 2.)

Do Thou our craven spirits cheer,
And shame away the selfish tear;
Sin only hides the genial ray,
And round the cross makes night of day.

FEBRUARY 2.

Morning:—

"Although the fig-tree shall not blossom,...yet I will rejoice in the Lord."—*Hab.* iii. 17, 18.

 Let the bright news of Jesus raise
  Our songs divinely high;
 And while our tongues repeat His praise,
  Let grief stand silent by.

Noon:—

"We are troubled on every side, yet NOT distressed."—2 *Cor.* iv. 8.

  These surface-troubles come and go,
   Like rufflings of the sea;
  The deeper depth is out of reach
   To all, my God, but Thee.

Evening:—

Do I suffer grief to overpower gratitude?—(*Eph.* v. 20.)

 O suffering Saviour, let me be
  Patient when crowding cares invade,
 Resign'd when earthly blessings flee,
  And grateful while enjoyments fade.

FEBRUARY 3.

Morning :—

"I will seek Him whom my soul loveth."—*S. Song* iii. 2.

> My life-long days would I still Thee
>   Be steadfastly beholding,
> Thee ever, as Thou ever me,
>   With loving arms enfolding.

Noon :—

"I love them that love Me."—*Prov.* viii. 17.

> Oh may we gaze upon Thy cross,
>   Until the wondrous sight
> Makes earthly treasures seem but dross,
>   And earthly sorrows light.

Evening :—

Do I love the Lord Jesus Christ?—(1 *Cor.* xvi. 22.)

> Do not I love Thee from my soul?
>   Then let me nothing love!
> Dead be my heart to every joy,
>   When Jesus cannot move.

FEBRUARY 4.

MORNING :—

"I will love Thee, O Lord my Strength."—*Psa.* xviii. 1.

> Thee will I love, my Strength, my Tower,
>   Thee will I love, my Joy, my Crown,
> Thee will I love with all my power,
>   In all Thy works, and Thee alone.

NOON :—

"Many waters cannot quench love, neither can the floods drown it."— *S. Song* viii. 7.

> But now I feel and know
> That only when we love, we find
> How far our hearts remain behind
> The love they should bestow.

EVENING :—

Is my love to Christ steadfast?— (*Rev.* ii. 4.)

> O gracious Shepherd, bind us
>   With cords of love to Thee ;
> And evermore remind us
>   How mercy set us free !

FEBRUARY 5.

MORNING :—

"Unto Thee, O my Strength, will I sing."—*Psa.* lix. 17.

> I know the power in whom I trust,
>   The arm on which I lean;
> Thou wilt my Saviour ever be,
>   Who hast my Saviour been.

NOON :—

"Christ is all and in all."—*Col.* iii. 11.

Take Him for strength and righteousness,
Make Him thy refuge in distress,
Love Him above all earthly joy,
And be His work thy glad employ.

EVENING :—

Do I seek to know more of the love which passeth knowledge?—(*Eph.* iii. 18, 19.)

> Thou King of light, our deepest longing
>   Is shallow to Thy depths of grace;
> Deep are the woes to us belonging,
>   But deeper far Thy joy to bless.

FEBRUARY 6.

MORNING:—

"The Lord is my portion;...therefore will I hope in Him."—*Lam.* iii. 24.

> Thou wert not born that earth should be
>   A portion fondly sought;
> Look up to heaven, and smiling see
>   Thy shining golden lot.

NOON:—

"The hope of the righteous shall be gladness."—*Prov.* x. 28.

> He comes, He comes, the Strong, to save!
>   He comes, nor tarries more!
> His light is breaking o'er the wave,
>   The clouds will soon be o'er!

EVENING:—

Do I hope in God's abounding mercy?—(*Jer.* iii. 23.)

> Trust in almighty grace and power;
>   Trust God's unerring skill;
> Trust Him in every clouded hour,
>   Against hope hoping still.

FEBRUARY 7.

MORNING:—

"My heart is fixed, O God, my heart is fixed; I will sing and give praise."—*Psa.* lvii. 7.

O happy day that fix'd my choice
  On Thee, my Saviour, and my God!
Well may this glowing heart rejoice,
  And tell its raptures all abroad.

NOON:—

"Blessed are they that keep My ways."—*Prov.* viii. 32.

Hosanna! Sovereign, Prophet, Priest!
  How vast Thy gifts, how free!
Thy blood our life, Thy word our feast,
  Thy name our only plea.

EVENING:—

Do I confide in God's almighty protection?—(*Psa.* xci. 1.)

Whom Thou dost guard, O King of kings,
  No evil shall molest;
Under the shadow of Thy wings
  Shall they securely rest.

FEBRUARY 8.

MORNING:—

"I will praise Thee, O Lord, with my whole heart."—*Psa.* ix. 1.

> Come, Thou Fount of every blessing,
>   Tune my heart to sing Thy grace;
> Streams of mercy never ceasing
>   Call for songs of loudest praise.

NOON:—

"The Lord shall...keep thy foot from being taken."—*Prov.* iii. 26.

> Father of love, our Guide and Friend,
>   Oh, gently lead us on,
> Until life's trial-time shall end,
>   And heavenly peace be won.

EVENING:—

Do I rejoice in God's watchful providence?—(*Psa.* xvi. 5.)

> O Thou, my light, my life, my joy,
>   My glory and my all,
> Unsent by Thee no good can come,
>   No evil can befall.

FEBRUARY 9.

MORNING:—

"The Lord is on my side; I will not fear: what can man do unto me?"—*Psa.* cxviii. 6.

> In God most holy, just, and true,
>   I have reposed my trust;
> Nor will I fear what man can do,
>   The offspring of the dust.

NOON:—

"Faint, yet pursuing."—*Judg.* viii. 4.

> Weak as you are, you shall not faint;
>   Or, fainting, shall not die;
> Jesus, the strength of every saint,
>   Shall aid you from on high.

EVENING:—

Am I a soldier of Christ Jesus?—(2 *Tim.* ii. 3.)

> Then let me meet my threefold foe,
> And conquering on to conquer go,
> Arm'd with His sword, and mind, and name,
> Who hell, the world, and sin o'ercame.

FEBRUARY 10.

MORNING :—

"Though war should rise against me, in this will I be confident."—*Psa.* xxvii. 3.

> Soldiers of Christ, arise,
>   And put your armour on;
> Strong in the strength which God supplies
>   Through His eternal Son.

NOON :—

"Chastened, and not killed."—2 *Cor.* vi. 9.

> Oh, cheer thee, cheer thee, suffering saint;
> Though worn with chastening, be not faint;
> And though thy night of pain seem long,
> Cling to thy Lord,—in Him be strong.

EVENING :—

Have I learned the secret of victory? —(1 *John* v. 4.)

> How will they live, how will they die,
>   How bear the cross of grief,
> Who have not found the light of faith,
>   The courage of belief?

FEBRUARY 11.

Morning :—

"My soul waiteth upon God;...He is my defence; I shall not be greatly moved."—*Psa*. lxii. 1, 2.

    Whoso, Lord, in Thee doth rest,
    He hath conquer'd, he is blest.

Noon :—

"Better it is to be of an humble spirit with the lowly, than to divide the spoil with the proud."—*Prov*. xvi. 19.

    Hide me safe within Thine arm,
    Where no foe can hurt or harm.

Evening :—

Am I prepared to meet the last enemy?—(1 *Cor*. xv. 26.)

Say to my soul, Be safe; and then mine eye
Shall scorn grim death, although grim death
    stand by;
Reach forth Thy hand, or bid me tread the
    wave,
I'll come, I'll come; the voice that calls will
    save.

FEBRUARY 12.

MORNING:—

"I will teach you the fear of the Lord."—*Psa.* xxxiv. 11.

   Praise that the young are brought
     His sacred truth to hear;
   And loftier praise that some are taught
     To worship in His fear.

NOON:—

"In him there is found SOME good thing."—1 *Kings* xiv. 13.

   And if SOME tones be false or low,
     What are all prayers beneath,
   But cries of babes that cannot know
     Half the deep thought they breathe!

EVENING:—

Do I believe that the seed of the righteous will be blessed?—(*Isa.* xliv. 3—5.)

   Through every scene of life and death,
     This promise is our trust;
   And this shall be our children's song
     When we are cold in dust.

FEBRUARY 13.

MORNING:—

"I will teach you by the hand of God."—*Job* xxvii. 11.

    Lord of the harvest, God of grace,
      Send down Thy heavenly rain;
    In vain we plant without Thine aid,
      And water too in vain.

NOON:—

"Whatsoever thy hand findeth to do, do it with thy might."—*Eccles.* ix. 10.

    Do what thou hast to do
      Before the night of gloom,
    That swiftly wraps the sons of men
      In darkness and the tomb.

EVENING:—

Do I pray for prayerless souls?—(*Ezek.* xxii. 30.)

    If some poor wandering child of Thine
    Have spurn'd to-day the voice divine,
    Now, Lord, the gracious work begin;
    Let him no more lie down in sin.

FEBRUARY 14.

MORNING:—

"My lips shall utter knowledge clearly."—*Job* xxxiii. 3.

> Be ever like earth's greatest, truest, soundest,
>   Be like the prophets of the prophet-land,
> Be like the Master,—simplest when profoundest;
>   So speak that fellow-men may understand.

NOON:—

"The commandment is a lamp, and the law is light."—*Prov.* vi. 23.

> How precious is the book divine,
>   By inspiration given!
> Bright as a lamp its doctrines shine,
>   To guide our souls to heaven.

EVENING:—

What am I the better for the light of Christ's gospel?—(1 *John* ii. 8—11.)

> To our benighted minds reveal
>   The glories of His grace;
> And bring us where no clouds conceal
>   The brightness of His face.

FEBRUARY 15.

MORNING:—

"We will walk in His paths."—*Isa.* ii. 3.

> The path may seem dark,
>   As He leads me along;
> But following Jesus,
>   I cannot go wrong.

NOON:—

"When thou runnest, thou shalt not stumble."—*Prov.* iv. 12.

> Show my forgetful feet the way
>   That leads to joys on high;
> There knowledge grows without decay,
>   And love shall never die.

EVENING:—

Am I willing to be made entirely holy?—(*Rom.* vii. 19.)

> Saviour, though my rebellious will
>   Has been by Thy blest grace renew'd,
> Yet in its secret workings still
>   How much remains to be subdued!

FEBRUARY 16.

MORNING:—

"Depart from me, ye evildoers; for I will keep the commandments of my God."—*Psa.* cxix. 115.

> Witness, ye men and angels, now;
> Before the Lord we speak;
> To Him we make our solemn vow,
> A vow we dare not break.

NOON:—

"Enter not into the path of the wicked."—*Prov.* iv. 14.

> 'Tis Thy will that we should be
> Separate from all around;
> Let our will with Thine agree,
> Let Thy people thus be found.

EVENING:—

Am I, like my Master, separate from sinners?—(*Heb.* vii. 26.)

> What sinners value, I resign;
> Lord, 'tis enough that Thou art mine;
> I shall behold Thy blissful face,
> And stand complete in righteousness.

FEBRUARY 17.

MORNING :—

"Mine eyes shall be upon the faithful of the land, that they may dwell with me."—*Psa.* ci. 6.

Thrice blest, whose lives are faithful prayers,
   Whose loves in higher love endure;
   What souls possess themselves so pure?
Or is there blessedness like theirs?

NOON:—

"Such as are upright in their way are His delight."—*Prov.* xi. 20.

The men that know Thy name will trust
   In Thine abundant grace;
For Thou dost ne'er forsake the just,
   Who humbly seek Thy face.

EVENING :—

Do I love the people of God?— (1 *John* v. 1.)

   My soul, to Jesus join'd
     By faith and hope and love,
   Now seeks to dwell among Thy saints,
     And rest with Thee above.

FEBRUARY 18.

MORNING:—

"Stablish Thy word unto Thy servant, who is DEVOTED to Thy fear."—*Psa.* cxix. 38.

> I rest upon Thy word,
> The promise is for me;
> My succour and salvation, Lord,
> Shall surely come from Thee.

NOON:—

"The desire of the righteous is only good."—*Prov.* xi. 23.

> Jesus, confirm my heart's desire
> To work, and speak, and think for Thee;
> Still let me guard the holy fire,
> And still stir up Thy gift in me.

EVENING:—

Am I a decided Christian?—(*Matt.* vi. 24.)

> Creatures, no more divide my choice:
> I bid you all depart;
> His name, and love, and gracious voice,
> Have fix'd my roving heart.

FEBRUARY 19.

Morning:—

"To me to live is Christ."—*Phil.*
i. 21.

Soon will the Lord my Life appear,
Soon shall I end my trials here;
Leave sin and sorrow, death and pain;—
To live is Christ,—to die is gain.

Noon:—

"The desire of the righteous shall be granted."—*Prov.* x. 24.

To Thy will I leave the rest,
Grant me but this one request,
Both in life and death to prove
Tokens of Thy special love.

Evening:—

Am I an energetic Christian?—
(1 *Cor.* xv. 10.)

Fountain of o'erflowing grace,
  Freely from Thy fulness give:
Till I close my earthly race,
  Be it "Christ" to me "to live."

FEBRUARY 20.

MORNING:—

"I give myself unto prayer."—*Psa.* cix. 4.

Long as our fiery trials last,
 Long as the cross we bear,
Oh, let our souls on Thee be cast
 In never-ceasing prayer.

NOON:—

"I will...that men pray everywhere, lifting up holy hands."—1 *Tim.* ii. 8.

Each place alike is holy ground,
 Where prayer from humble souls is pour'd,
Where praise awakes its silver sound,
 Or God is silently adored.

EVENING:—

Am I a prayerful Christian?—(*Luke* xviii. 1.)

The heartfelt sigh, the tearful word,
The fervent prayer shall still be heard;
Rich floods of heavenly grace descend,
And blessings that shall know no end.

FEBRUARY 21.

Morning:—

"Let us exalt His name together."
—*Psa.* xxxiv. 3.

> Praise Him, all ye heavenly choirs,
> Praise, and sweep your golden lyres!
> Shout, O earth, in rapturous song;
> Let the strains be sweet and strong.

Noon:—

"Bless the Lord, ye His angels; ye ministers of His, that do His pleasure."
—*Psa.* ciii. 20.

> Angelic powers, seraphic flames,
> Proclaim aloud the glorious names
> Of God the Saviour and the Just,
> The sinner's dread, his surest trust.

Evening:—

Is the Lord Jesus my Saviour and Friend?—(*Acts* iii. 26.)

> For ever His dear sacred name
>   Shall dwell upon our tongue,
> And Jesus and salvation be
>   The close of every song.

FEBRUARY 22.

Morning:—

"We have waited for Him; we will be glad and rejoice in His salvation."
—*Isa.* xxv. 9.

> Awake, our love; awake, our joy;
> Awake, our heart and tongue;
> Sleep not when mercies loudly call;
> Break forth into a song.

Noon:—

"Sing unto the Lord, O ye saints of His."—*Psa.* xxx. 4.

> Rejoice, ye sons of God, rejoice,
> And doubt His love no more;
> Lift up your hearts, lift up your voice,
> And His rich grace adore.

Evening:—

Is Christ's presence my highest joy?
—(*Luke* xxiv. 29.)

> Jesus, Thy presence I implore;
> This blessing now bestow;
> With me abide, nor leave me more,
> While I remain below.

FEBRUARY 23.

MORNING:—

"We, Thy people, and sheep of Thy pasture, will give Thee thanks."—*Psa.* lxxix. 13.

> Who can have greater cause to sing,
> Who greater cause to bless,
> Than we, the children of a King,
> Than we, who Christ possess!

NOON:—

"Let everything that hath breath praise the Lord."—*Psa.* cl. 6.

> Nearest the throne, and first in song,
> Man shall his hallelujahs raise,
> While wondering angels round him throng,
> And swell the chorus of His praise.

EVENING:—

Is Christ's life my pattern?—(1 *Pet.* ii. 21.)

> How shall I follow Him I serve?
> How shall I copy Him I love?
> Nor from those blessed footsteps swerve,
> Which lead me to His seat above?

FEBRUARY 24.

Morning:—

"If he...oweth thee ought,...I will repay it."—*Philem.* 18, 19.

> Happy is he that fears the Lord,
>   And follows His commands,
> Who lends the poor without reward,
>   Or gives with liberal hands.

Noon:—

"Rejoice with them that do rejoice, and weep with them that weep."—*Rom.* xii. 15.

> Oh, may our sympathizing breasts
>   With generous feelings glow,
> Kindly to share in others' joy,
>   Or weep with others' we.

Evening:—

Does love reign in my heart?—(1 *John* iv. 16.)

> Love is the theme of saints above,
>   Love be the theme of saints below;
> Love is of God, for God is Love;
>   With love let every bosom glow.

FEBRUARY 25.

MORNING:—

"I will very gladly spend and be spent for you."—2 *Cor.* xii. 15.

    I would the precious time redeem,
        And longer live for this alone,
    To spend and to be spent for them
        Who have not yet my Saviour known.

NOON:—

"Bear ye one another's burdens, and so fulfil the law of Christ."—*Gal.* vi. 2.

    Thus passing through the vale of tears
        Our useful light shall shine,
    And others learn to glorify
        Our Father's name divine.

EVENING:—

Does love rule my actions?—(1 *John* iii. 18.)

    The heart—the heart—that's truly blest
        Is never all its own;
    No ray of glory lights the breast
        That beats for self alone.

FEBRUARY 26.

MORNING :—

"I will not...offer burnt-offerings without cost."—1 *Chron.* xxi. 24.

Largely Thou givest, gracious Lord,
Largely Thy gifts should be restored;
Freely Thou givest, and Thy word
   Is,—Freely give.

NOON :—

"I the Lord love judgment, I hate robbery for burnt-offering."— *Isa.* lxi. 8.

And what have hypocrites to do
   To bring their sacrifice?
They call My statutes just and true,
   But deal in theft and lies.

EVENING :—

Does love prompt my offerings?— (1 *Cor.* xiii. 3.)

Our souls and bodies we resign
   To fear and follow Thy commands;
Oh! take our hearts,—our hearts are Thine,
   Accept the tribute of our hands.

FEBRUARY 27.

MORNING :—

"Unto Thee will I cry, O Lord my Rock."—*Psa.* xxviii. 1.

> From darkness here and weariness
> We ask not full repose;
> Only be Thou at hand to bless
> Our trial-hour of woes.

NOON :—

"Be not afraid; only believe."—*Mark* v. 36.

> When we in darkness walk,
> Nor feel the heavenly flame,
> Then is the time to trust our God,
> And rest upon His name.

EVENING :—

Do my afflictions lead me to God's footstool?—(*Psa.* l. 15.)

> Behold me here in grief draw near,
> Pleading at Thy throne, O King!
> To Thee each tear, each trembling fear,
> Jesus, Son of man, I bring!

FEBRUARY 23.

MORNING:—

"In Thy fear will I worship toward Thy holy temple."—*Psa.* v. 7.

> Be Thou near us, blessed Saviour,
>   Still at morn and eve the same;
> Give us faith that cannot waver,
>   Kindle in us Heaven's own flame.

NOON:—

"Lord, I believe; help Thou mine unbelief."—*Mark* ix. 24.

> When we leave the heights of Tabor
>   For earth's valleys dim and cold,
> Through life's toil, and care, and labour,
>   Only Jesus can uphold.

EVENING:—

Do I ever rise above the sorrows of earth?—(2 *Cor.* iv. 18.)

> Sometimes I climb a little way,
>   And thence look down below;
> How nothing there do all things seem
>   That here make such a show!

FEBRUARY 29.

MORNING:—

"I will dwell in the house of the Lord for ever."—*Psa*. xxiii. 6.

O the bright hope! my soul, be strong!
Soon wilt thou join the endless song,
Enter those courts so fair, so bright,
That temple which the Lamb doth light.

NOON:—

"The righteous is delivered out of trouble."—*Prov*. xi. 8.

With patience wait awhile
 The issue of thy woes,
Soon shall the desert smile
 And blossom like the rose.

EVENING:—

Do I seek to realize even present good from my trials?—(2 *Cor*. iv. 16.)

Seems it long till purple morning
 Streaks the eastern sky with light?
Stars with beauty are adorning
 E'en the sable brow of night.

MARCH 1.

MORNING:—

"If the Lord will, we shall live, and do this, or that."—*Jam.* iv. 15.

> Our residue of days or hours
>   Thine, wholly Thine, shall be;
> And all our consecrated powers
>   A sacrifice to Thee.

NOON:—

"Boast not thyself of to-morrow."—*Prov.* xxvii. 1.

> Watch, for thou know'st not of the time
>   The Lord will come with mighty power,
> Whether at day's unsullied prime,
>   At early dawn, or midnight hour.

EVENING:—

Am I disquieted about my future welfare?—(*Matt.* vi. 33.)

> Live for to-day; to-morrow's light
> To-morrow's cares shall bring to sight;
> Go, sleep like closing flowers at night,
>   And Heaven thy morn will bless.

MARCH 2.

Morning:—

"In all things willing to live honestly."—*Heb.* xiii. 18.

    Let those who bear the Christian name
        Their holy vows fulfil;
    The saints, the followers of the Lamb,
        Are men of honour still.

Noon:—

"The highway of the upright is to depart from evil; he that keepeth his way preserveth his soul." *Prov.* xvi. 17.

    The trivial round, the common task,
    Will furnish all we ought to ask,
    Room to deny ourselves, a road
    To bring us daily nearer God.

Evening:—

Am I contented with my present lot?—(1 *Tim.* vi. 8.)

    Not mine, not mine the choice,
        In things or great or small;
    Be Thou my Guide, my Strength,
        My Wisdom, and my All.

MARCH 3.

MORNING :—

"We will deal kindly and truly with thee."—*Josh.* ii. 14.

Small service is true service while it lasts;
  Of friends, however humble, scorn not one;
The daisy, by the shadow that it casts,
  Protects the lingering dewdrop from the sun.

NOON :—

"A friend loveth at all times, and a brother is born for adversity."—*Prov.* xvii. 17.

  With pity let my breast o'erflow
  When I behold a brother's wo;
  And bear a sympathizing part
  Whene'er I meet a wounded heart.

EVENING :—

Am I grateful for past mercies?—(*Phil.* iv. 10.)

  Oh, to live exempt from care
  By the energy of prayer;
  Strong in faith, with mind subdued,
  Yet elate with gratitude.

MARCH 4.

MORNING:—

"Lord, I will follow Thee."—*Luke* ix. 61.

> Be Thou our guide; be Thou our goal;
> Be Thou our pathway to the skies;
> Our joy, when sorrow fills the soul;
> In death, our everlasting prize.

NOON:—

"In the way of righteousness is life."—*Prov.* xii. 28.

> To gain the height of Zion's hill
> I would with fervour strive,
> And all those powers devote to Thee
> Which I from Thee derive.

EVENING:—

In what way am I called to follow Christ?—(*Matt.* xx. 22.)

> Thou art our Pattern to the end of time,
> O Crucified! and perfect is Thy will;
> The workers follow Thee in doing good;
> The weepers think of Calvary, and are still.

MARCH 5.

MORNING :—

"I have CHOSEN Thy precepts."—
Psa. cxix. 173.

> Let fools my wiser choice deride,
> Angels and God approve;
> Nor scorn of men, nor rage of hell,
> My steadfast soul shall move.

NOON :—

"I am Thine; save me; for I have sought Thy precepts."—*Psa.* cxix. 94.

> Why should the world presume
> To occupy Thy throne?
> Come, all Thy right assume,
> I would be Thine alone.

EVENING :—

Am I discouraged by my own weakness?—(*Phil.* iv. 13.)

> Saviour, to Thy love we fly;
> On that love our souls rely.
> Friend unfailing, Friend Divine,
> Oh, what constancy is Thine!

MARCH 6.

MORNING:—

"Though all men shall be offended because of Thee, yet will I never be offended."—*Matt.* xxvi. 33.

Ashamed of Jesus?—that dear Friend,
On whom my hopes of heaven depend?
No! when I blush, be this my shame,
That I no more revere His name.

NOON:—

"If thou faint in the day of adversity, thy strength is small."—*Prov.* xxiv. 10.

Oh, weak to know a Saviour's power,
  To feel a Father's care!
A moment's toil, a passing shower,
  Is all the grief ye share.

EVENING:—

Is affliction a stumbling-block to me?—(1 *Thess.* iii. 3.)

To Thee more closely may we cling
  In every new distress;
Thy word the sweetest peace can bring,
  Thy Spirit truly bless.

MARCH 7.

MORNING :—

"I will sing unto the Lord;...He hath dealt bountifully with me." *Psa.* xiii. 6.

Didst Thou bless me, didst Thou chasten,
   With Thy smile, or with Thy rod,
'Twas that still my steps might hasten
   Homeward, heavenward, to my God.

NOON :—

"The foolishness of man perverteth his way, and his heart fretteth against the Lord."—*Prov.* xix. 3.

Oh, why should I murmur and grieve,
   Since my Shepherd is always the same,
And has promised He never will leave
   The soul that confides in His name!

EVENING :—

Have I the light of gospel-hope?— (2 *Tim.* i. 10.)

Though dark and lonely be our way,
   A thousand stars shine sweetly o'er us,
And immortality's pure ray
   Gladdens and gilds the path before us.

MARCH 8.

Morning :—

"I will bless the Lord, who hath given me counsel."—*Psa.* xvi. 7.

God of my life, through all my days,
My grateful powers shall speak Thy praise;
My song shall wake with opening light,
And cheer the dark and silent night.

Noon :—

"The Spirit itself beareth witness with our spirit."—*Rom.* viii. 16.

There is a gentle inner voice
  That calms us in our saddest hour,
And bids us in a hope rejoice
  Beyond the reach of this world's power.

Evening :—

Have I the Spirit's guidance?—(*Rom.* viii. 14.)

Oh, make Thy precepts sweet to me
  By Thy good Spirit's gentle sway;
And let my feet be led by Thee
  In Thine own true and perfect way.

MARCH 9.

MORNING:—

"My meditation of Him shall be sweet."—*Psa.* civ. 34.

> Here fix, my roving heart,
>   Here wait, my warmest love,
> Till the communion be complete
>   In nobler scenes above.

NOON:—

"I saw the holy city, new Jerusalem."—*Rev.* xxi. 2.

> There is a golden city
>   Beyond the bridgeless river,
> And all the blest, who find its rest,
>   Shall dwell in joy for ever.

EVENING:—

Have I a believing view of the Celestial City?—(*Heb.* xi. 10.)

> Short the space, and He will take us
>   To Himself,—oh! wondrous love!
> And of His great glory make us
>   Sharers in the realms above.

MARCH 10.

MORNING:—

"I will walk at liberty, for I seek Thy precepts."—*Psa.* cxix. 45.

> Serene will be our days and bright,
> And happy will our nature be,
> When love is an unerring light,
> And joy its own security.

NOON:—

"Where the Spirit of the Lord is, there is liberty."—2 *Cor.* iii. 17.

> Oh, what a blessedness sublime,
> True life to realize,
> To walk amid the things of Time,
> In commerce with the skies.

EVENING:—

Am I freed from the yoke of bondage?—(*Gal.* v. 1.)

> In a service which Thy love appoints
> There are no bonds for me;
> For my secret heart is taught the truth
> That makes Thy children "free."

MARCH 11.

MORNING :—

"I will keep Thy precepts with my whole heart."—*Psa.* cxix. 69.

>Oh, help me, Lord, in Thine own strength
>   This purpose to fulfil;
>And onward lead, till I at length
>   Stand perfect in Thy will.

NOON :—

"The way of the Lord is strength to the upright."—*Prov.* x. 29.

>When life her throng of cares reveals,
>And weakness o'er my spirit steals,
>Grateful I hear the kind decree,
>That, as my days, my strength shall be.

EVENING :—

Do I make a right use of my Christian liberty?—(*Gal.* v. 13.)

>Jesus, I hide my head in shame,
>   I blush and weep to see
>That I, who bear Thy sacred name,
>   No more conform to Thee.

MARCH 12.

Morning:—

"I will run the way of Thy commandments, when Thou shalt enlarge my heart."—*Psa.* cxix. 32.

> Are not Thy mercies sovereign still?
> And Thou a faithful God?
> Wilt Thou not grant me warmer zeal
> To run the heavenly road?

Noon:—

"Blessings are upon the head of the just."—*Prov.* x. 6.

> To rest on Thee alone,
> And feel Thy power to bless,
> To live and die Thine own,
> This, this is happiness.

Evening:—

Do I realize my Christian privileges?—(*Gal.* iv. 6, 7.)

> Why should the children of a King
> Go mourning all their days?
> Great Comforter, descend and bring
> Some tokens of Thy grace.

MARCH 13.

MORNING :—

"My tongue shall speak of Thy righteousness and of Thy praise all the day long."—*Psa.* xxxv. 28.

> Thy grace can lift each drooping head,
> Thy power all means employ;
> About Thy footsteps light is shed;
> Around Thy dealings, joy.

NOON :—

"He heareth the prayer of the righteous."—*Prov.* xv. 29.

> Boundless wisdom, power divine,
> Love unspeakable, are Thine;
> Wisdom, Lord, to me be given,
> Wisdom pure which comes from heaven.

EVENING :—

Do I rejoice in God's pardoning love?—(*Acts* xvi. 34.)

> He passes all our follies by,
> And all our sins forgives;
> His wrath doth in a moment die,
> His love for ever lives.

MARCH 14.

MORNING :—

"My tongue shall sing ALOUD of Thy righteousness."—*Psa.* li. 14.

> Awake, ye saints, and raise your eyes,
>   And lift your voices high;
> Extol the sovereign love that shows
>   Our full redemption nigh.

NOON :—

"He giveth grace unto the lowly."
—*Prov.* iii. 34.

> Millions of happy spirits live
>   On Thine exhaustless store,
> From Thee they all their bliss receive,
>   And still Thou givest more.

EVENING :—

Do I thirst after God's presence?—(*Psa.* xlii. 1.)

> No voice but Thine can give me rest,
>   And bid my fears depart;
> No love but Thine can make me blest,
>   And satisfy my heart.

MARCH 15.

MORNING:—

"Thus will I bless Thee while I live."—*Psa*. lxiii. 4.

I'll lift my hands, I'll raise my voice,
    While I have breath to pray or praise;
This work shall make my heart rejoice,
    And fill the remnant of my days.

NOON:—

"A man's heart deviseth his way; but the Lord directeth his steps."—*Prov.* xvi. 9.

What though He let thee not perform
    Some good and loved design?
Thou wouldst not wish Him to conform
    His perfect will to thine!

EVENING:—

Do I submit to God's will?—(*Acts* xxi. 14.)

Thy ways, O Lord, with wise design,
    Are framed upon Thy throne above;
And every dark and bending line
    Meets in the centre of Thy love.

MARCH 16.

MORNING :—

"Who will go for us? then said I, Here am I, send me."—*Isa*. vi. 8.

> The Master whom you serve
>   Will needful strength bestow;
> Depending on His promised aid,
>   With sacred courage go.

NOON :—

"He that winneth souls is wise."—*Prov*. xi. 30.

> Let love its angel-hand extend
>   To those who linger in the plain,
> With gentle care their steps befriend,
>   Till Zoar's safe refuge they attain.

EVENING :—

Is work for Christ a pleasure to me?—(1 *Cor*. ix. 17.)

> Come, Lord, when grace has made me meet,
>   Thy blessed face to see,
> For if Thy work on earth be sweet,
>   What will Thy glory be?

MARCH 17.

MORNING:—

"So, as much as in me is, I am ready to preach the Gospel."—*Rom.* i. 15.

> Suppress my shame, subdue my fear,
>   Arm me with heavenly zeal,
> That I may make Thy power appear,
>   And works of praise fulfil.

NOON:—

"Be not thou...ashamed of the testimony of our Lord."—2 *Tim.* i. 8.

> I'm not ashamed to own my Lord,
>   Or to defend His cause,
> Maintain the honour of His word,
>   The glory of His cross.

EVENING:—

Is the gospel of Christ my treasure?—(*Rom.* i. 16.)

> Thanks we give, and adoration,
>   For Thy gospel's joyful sound;
> May the fruits of Thy salvation
>   In our hearts and lives abound.

MARCH 18.

Morning:—

"I seek not Mine own will, but the will of the Father."—*John* v. 30.

> Be my All;—whate'er I do,
>   Let me only seek Thy will.
> Where the heart to Thee is true,
>   All is peaceful, calm, and still.

Noon:—

"The counsel of the Lord, that shall stand."—*Prov.* xix. 21.

> Let Him alone the world control;
>   None wiser reigns than He;
> The dealings of His hand, thy soul
>   With wondering eye shall see.

Evening:—

Does the peace of God dwell in my heart?—(*Phil.* iv. 7.)

> Straight to my home above
>   I travel calmly on,
> And sing in life or death,
>   My Lord, Thy will be done.

MARCH 19.

MORNING :—

"Let us lift up our heart with our hands unto God in the heavens."— *Lam.* iii. 41.

    Almighty Father, hearken,
      Forgive, and help, and bless,
    Nor let Thine anger darken
      The night of our distress.

NOON :—

"The just shall come out of trouble." —*Prov.* xii. 13.

Art thou a pilgrim, and alone,
Far from the home once called thine own?
Thy life a cheerless wintry day,
Unlit by sunshine?—Rise and pray!

EVENING :—

Do I feel the need of prayer?— (*Ezek.* xxxvi. 37.)

    Oh, help us when our spirits bleed
      In contrite anguish sore;
    And when our hearts are cold and dead,
      Oh, help us, Lord, the more.

MARCH 20.

MORNING:—

"Quicken us, and we will call upon Thy name."—*Psa.* lxxx. 18.

High as Thou art, Thou still art near
　When suppliants succour crave;
And as Thine ear is swift to hear,
　Thine arm is strong to save.

NOON:—

"The sacrifice of the wicked is an abomination to the Lord." *Prov.* xv. 8.

One thing alone, dear Lord, I dread,
　To have a secret spot,
That separates my soul from Thee,
　And yet to know it not.

EVENING:—

Do I pray away all hindrances to prayer?—(*Isa.* lix. 2.)

If gloom thy soul enshroud,
　If tears faith's eye bedim,
If doubts around thee crowd,
　Come, tell them all to Him.

MARCH 21.

MORNING:—

"We will give ourselves continually to prayer."—*Acts* vi. 4.

> Jesus, if Thou withdraw Thy hand,
>   That moment sees me fall;
> Oh, may I ne'er on self depend,
>   But look to Thee for all.

NOON:—

"The prayer of the upright is His delight."—*Prov.* xv. 8.

> I love, when tried and tempted,
>   Beset with doubts and fears,
> To cast my care on Jesus;
>   He wipes away my tears.

EVENING:—

Do I know the blessedness of prayer?—(*James* v. 16.)

> Blest hour, when God Himself draws nigh,
>   Well pleased His people's voice to hear,
> To list the penitential sigh,
>   And wipe away the mourner's tear.

MARCH 22.

MORNING :—

"I will incline mine ear to a parable."—*Psa.* xlix. 4.

> Now let our darkness comprehend
>   The light that shines so clear;
> Now the revealing Spirit send,
>   And give us ears to hear.

NOON :—

"Never man spake like this Man."—*John* vii. 46.

> How sweetly flow'd the gospel's sound
>   From lips of gentleness and grace,
> While listening thousands gather'd round,
>   And joy and reverence fill'd the place.

EVENING :—

As a learner, am I attentive?—(*James* i. 19.)

> Great God, Thy sovereign power impart,
>   To grant Thy word success;
> Write Thy salvation in my heart,
>   And make me learn Thy grace.

MARCH 23.

Morning :—

"I will open my mouth in a parable."
—*Psa*. lxxviii. 2.

What memory stores, what faith can reach,
With grace and wisdom may we teach;
Unto the simple gladly bend,
And be to all the guide and friend.

Noon :—

"Surely my judgment is with the Lord, and my work with my God."—*Isa*. xlix. 4.

Oh, if for our unworthiness,
  Toil, prayer, and watching fail,
In disappointment Thou canst bless,
  So love at heart prevail.

Evening :—

As a sufferer, am I patient?—(*Luke* xxi. 19.)

If works of faith, and labours sweet of love,
May not be mine, yet patient hope can be
Within my heart, like a bright censer's fire,
With incense of thanksgiving mounting free.

MARCH 24.

MORNING:—

"I will not dare to speak of any of those things which Christ hath not wrought by me."—*Rom.* xv. 18.

    And if the love of a grateful heart
      As a rich reward be given,
    Lift thou the love of a grateful heart
      To the God of love in heaven.

NOON:—

"Before honour is humility." *Prov.* xv. 33.

The saint that wears heaven's brightest crown,
    In deepest adoration bends;
The weight of glory bows him down,
    Then most, when most his soul ascends.

EVENING:—

As a teacher, am I humble?—(1 *Tim.* iii. 6.)

    [Good Lord], our pride repress,
    And give us grace, a growing store,
    That day by day we may do more,
      And still esteem it less.

MARCH 25.

MORNING:—

"I will declare what He hath done for my soul."—*Psa.* lxvi. 16.

 Grace taught my wandering feet,
  To tread the heavenly road;
 And new supplies each hour I meet,
  While pressing on to God.

NOON:—

"Come and hear all ye that fear God."—*Psa.* lxvi. 16.

 Come, and rejoice with me,
  For I was wearied sore,
 And I have found a mighty arm
  Which holds me evermore.

EVENING:—

Do I delight to speak and hear of Jesus?—(1 *Pet.* ii. 7.)

 Precious is the name of Jesus;
  Who can half its worth unfold?
 Far beyond angelic praises,
  Sweetly sung to harps of gold!

MARCH 26.

MORNING :—

"If I must needs glory, I will glory of the things which concern mine infirmities."—2 *Cor.* xi. 30.

> We love the stroke that breaks our chain,
> The sword by which our sins are slain;
> And while abased in dust we bow,
> We sing the grace that lays us low.

NOON :—

"These are they which came out of great tribulation."—*Rev.* vii. 14.

> Oh, what are all my sufferings here,
>   If, Lord, Thou count me meet
> With that enraptured host to appear
>   And worship at Thy feet.

EVENING :—

Is Jesus my strength, my song, my salvation?—(*Isa.* li. 11.)

> Through all the path I'll sing His name,
>   Till I the mount ascend,
> Where toils and storms are known no more,
>   And anthems never end.

MARCH 27.

MORNING:—

"My soul shall make her boast in the Lord."—*Psa.* xxxiv. 2.

> To Thee, my God and Saviour,
> My heart exulting sings,
> Rejoicing in Thy favour,
> Almighty King of kings.

NOON:—

"The way of the righteous is made plain."—*Prov.* xv. 19.

> Our God unfolds by slow degrees
> The purpose of His deep decrees;
> But spreads at length before the soul
> A beautiful and perfect whole.

EVENING:—

Is Christ in me, the hope of glory?
—(*Col.* i. 27.)

> From the first breath of life divine
> Down to my last expiring hour,
> The work of love must all be Thine,
> Begun and ended by Thy power.

MARCH 28.

MORNING :—

"I will bless the Lord at ALL times."
—*Psa.* xxxiv. 1.

Thou art, O God, the life and light
   Of all this wondrous world we see;
Its glow by day, its smile by night,
   Are but reflections caught from Thee.

NOON :—

"Remember now thy Creator."—
Eccles. xii. 1.

Lord, raise my faith, my hope, my heart,
   To heaven's transporting joys,
Then shall I shun each fatal snare
   Which this vain world employs.

EVENING :—

Do I prize the light of Revelation above that of Nature?—(*Psa.* cxix. 64.)

The heavens declare Thy glory, Lord;
   In every star Thy wisdom shines;
But when our eyes behold Thy word,
   We read Thy name in fairer lines.

MARCH 29.

MORNING :—

"I will sing unto the Lord as long as I live."—*Psa*. civ. 33.

> The creature of Thy hand,
> By Thee alone I live;
> My God, Thy benefits demand
> More praise than life can give.

NOON :—

"Fear God and keep His commandments."—*Eccles*. xii. 13.

> My Saviour, till my life shall end,
> Be Thou my Counsellor and Friend,
> Teach me Thy precepts all divine,
> And be Thy great example mine.

EVENING :—

What if this night my soul were required of me?—(*Luke* xii. 20.)

> My soul, or meditate the dread,
> Or else indulge the joy,
> Until the praise of love divine
> Thy sweetest thoughts employ.

MARCH 30.

MORNING:—

"I will sing of the mercies of the Lord FOR EVER."—*Psa.* lxxxix. 1.

Wonders of grace and power
  To Thee alone belong;
Thy Church those wonders shall adore
  In everlasting song.

NOON:—

"My delights were with the sons of men."—*Prov.* viii. 31.

Eternal God, our wondering souls
  Admire Thy matchless grace,
That Thou wilt walk, that Thou wilt dwell,
  With Adam's worthless race.

EVENING:—

Are my lips tuned to holy song?—(*Col.* iii. 16.)

Whilst I His gracious succour prove
  Midst all my various ways,
The darkest shades through which I pass
  Shall echo with His praise.

MARCH 31.

MORNING :—

"I will freely sacrifice unto Thee."
—*Psa.* liv. 6.

> Lord, Thou hast died!
> This hast Thou done for me!
> What have I done for Thee,
>   Thou Crucified?

NOON :—

"My son, fear thou the Lord."—
Prov. xxiv. 21.

> See, He comes to meet thee, sealing
>   With His own most holy word
> Pardon, blessing, strength, and healing;
>   Turn! oh, turn thee to the Lord!

EVENING :—

Have I this day made any sacrifice for God?—(*Mark* x. 28.)

> Were the whole realm of nature mine,
>   That were a present far too small;
> Love so amazing, so divine,
>   Demands my soul, my life, my all.

APRIL 1.

Morning:—
"I will pay Thee my vows."—*Psa.* lxvi. 13.

> As endless ages roll along,
> Endless shall be my grateful song;
> And heaven itself shall pass away
> Before I cease my vows to pay.

Noon:—
"Better is it that thou shouldest not vow, than that thou shouldest vow, and not pay."—*Eccles.* v. 5.

> Weak and irresolute is man;
>   The purpose of to-day,
> Woven with pains into his plan,
>   To-morrow rends away.

Evening:—
Have I been steadfast in the covenant?—(*Psa.* lxxviii. 10, 37.)

> Lord, as to Thy dear cross we flee,
>   And plead to be forgiven,
> So let Thy life our pattern be,
>   And form our souls for heaven.

APRIL 2.

MORNING:—

"My praise shall be of Thee in the great congregation."—*Psa.* xxii. 25.

> O praise ye the Lord!
> Prepare a new song!
> With voices united
> The anthem prolong!

NOON:—

"Whoso trusteth in the Lord, happy is he."—*Prov.* xvi. 20.

> Our Faith shall look through every tear,
> And view Thy smiling face;
> And Hope, amidst our sighs, shall tune
> An anthem to Thy grace.

EVENING:—

Do I value Christ as an unchanging Saviour?—(*Heb.* xiii. 8.)

> I change, He changes not;
> The Christ can never die;
> His love, not mine, the resting-place;
> His truth, not mine, the tie.

APRIL 3.

MORNING:—

"Teach me, O Lord, the way of Thy statutes, and I shall keep it unto the end."—*Psa.* cxix. 33.

> Faith, by the Word begotten,
> Doth by the Word increase,
> Before the Word bows humbly,
> And in the Word finds peace.

NOON:—

"Whoso hearkeneth unto Me, shall dwell safely."—*Prov.* i. 33.

The covenant of grace all blessings secures;
Believer, rejoice, for all things are yours;
And God from His purpose will never remove,
But love thee, and bless thee, and rest in His love.

EVENING:—

Have I learned in everything to give thanks?—(1 *Thess.* v. 18.)

> Toil, trial, suffering, still await
>   On earth the pilgrim throng,
> Yet learn we in our low estate
>   The Church triumphant's song.

APRIL 4.

MORNING:—

"I will wait upon the Lord, that hideth His face...and I will look for Him."—*Isa.* viii. 17.

> For His deep coming watch
>   With listening heart of prayer;
> And ever lift the inward latch,
>   That bids Him entrance there.

NOON:—

"Those that seek Me early shall find Me."—*Prov.* viii. 17.

> We kneel, and all around us seems to lower!
> We rise, and all,—the distant and the near,—
> Stands forth in sunny outline, brave and clear!
> We kneel, how weak! we rise, how full of
>   power!

EVENING:—

Have I learned at all times to hope?
—(*Lam.* iii. 21.)

> Though thou think Him far away,
>   Though His mercy long have slept,
> He will come and not delay,
>   When His child enough hath wept.

APRIL 5.

MORNING :—

"I will say of the Lord, He is my Refuge and my Fortress: my God; in Him will I trust."—*Psa*. xci. 2.

My Strength, my Shield, my safe Abode,
My Priest before the throne of God,
In death, as life, be Thou my Guide,
And save me, who for me hast died.

NOON :—

"Whoso findeth Me, findeth life."
—*Prov*. viii. 35.

Let good or ill befall,
It must be good for me,
Secure of having Thee in all,
Of having all in Thee.

EVENING :—

Have I learned with all things to be content?—(*Phil*. iv. 11, 12.)

Oh! tell me, Lord, that Thou art mine,
What can I wish beside?
My soul shall at the fountain live,
When all the streams are dried.

APRIL 6.

MORNING:—

"The Lord our God will we serve, and His voice will we obey."—*Josh.* xxiv. 24.

To-day we hear our Shepherd's voice,
   And gladly answer to the call;
In Him unseen our hearts rejoice,
   Who knows, and names, and loves us all.

NOON:—

"Take heed what ye do."—2 *Chron.* xix. 6.

We spend our midday sweat, our midnight oil,
We tire the night in thought, the day in toil,
To compass earth, and with her empty store
To fill our arms, and grasp one handful more.

EVENING:—

Have I this day been guilty of self-worship?—(*Phil.* ii. 21.)

   Has not my resolution fail'd?
     Lord, search, for Thou didst see!
   And has not base self-love prevail'd
     Instead of love to Thee?

APRIL 7.

MORNING :—

"We will not...worship the golden image."—*Dan.* iii. 18.

Be dead, my heart, to worldly charms;
  Be dead to every sin;
And tell the boldest foes without,
  That Jesus reigns within.

NOON :—

"Labour not to be rich; cease from thine own wisdom."—*Prov.* xxiii. 4.

One little moment can destroy
  Our vast laborious schemes,
And all our heaps of solid joy
  Are sweet deceitful dreams.

EVENING :—

Have I indulged in mammon-worship?—(*Luke* xvi. 13—15.)

Oh, what this world to thee, my heart?
  Its gifts nor feed thee, nor can bless;
Thou hast no owner's part
  In all its nothingness.

APRIL 8.

MORNING :—

"Neither will we say any more to the work of our hands, Ye are our gods."—*Hos.* xiv. 3.

    Oh, when will man be taught
      The truth of history's tale,
    That all by mortals wrought
      Is brief,—as they are frail!

NOON :—

"The price of wisdom is above rubies."—*Job* xxviii. 18.

    Oft in Thy house Thy glory shines
      Before our wondering eyes;
    We wish not THEN for golden mines,
      Or aught beneath the skies.

EVENING :—

Am I guilty of any secret idolatry? —(1 *John* v. 21.)

    The dearest idol I have known,
      Whate'er that idol be,
    Help me to tear it from Thy throne,
      And worship only Thee.

APRIL 9.

MORNING:—

"I will extol Thee, my God, O King."—*Psa.* cxlv. 1.

> Oh, worship the King
> All glorious above;
> Oh, gratefully sing
> His power and His love.

NOON:—

"Rejoice evermore; pray without ceasing."—1 *Thess.* v. 16, 17.

> My thoughts address His throne,
> When morning brings the light;
> I seek His blessing every noon;
> And pay my vows at night.

EVENING:—

Do I serve God with joy and gladness?—(*Psa.* c. 2.)

Thy brow wears trace of suffering; thy soul's lute
Hath lost its melody, and joy is mute;
  Yet gaze above!
Thy Saviour liveth, and His name is Love.

APRIL 10.

MORNING :—

"I will speak of the glorious honour of Thy majesty."—*Psa.* cxlv. 5.

My God, how wonderful Thou art!
Thy majesty, how bright!
How radiant Thy mercy-seat,
In depths of burning light!

NOON :—

"Serve the Lord with fear, and rejoice with trembling."—*Psa.* ii. 11.

Rejoice with trembling, mourn with hope,
Take life as life is given;
Its rough ascent, its flowery slope,
May lead alike to heaven.

EVENING :—

Do I serve God with reverence?—(*Heb.* xii. 28.)

Who know His power,
His grace who prove,
Serve Him with awe,
With reverence love.

APRIL 11.

Morning:—

"My tongue shall speak of Thy word."—*Psa.* cxix. 172.

> Great God, with wonder and with praise
>   On all Thy works I look;
> But still Thy wisdom, power, and grace
>   Shine brightest in Thy book.

Noon:—

"Thou knowest not what a day may bring forth."—*Prov.* xxvii. 1.

> This day, may every hour correct
>   The follies of the past;
> And such may all its actions be,
>   As would adorn my last.

Evening:—

Do I serve the holy God with holiness of heart and life?—(*Luke* i. 74, 75.)

> May deep repentance, faith, and love,
>   Be join'd with godly fear;
> And all our conversation prove
>   Our hearts to be sincere.

APRIL 12.

MORNING:—

"I have borne chastisement; I will not offend any more."—*Job* xxxiv. 31.

    Kind, loving is the hand that strikes,
      However keen the smart,
    If sorrow's discipline can chase
      One evil from the heart.

NOON:—

"Apply thine heart unto instruction."—*Prov.* xxiii. 12.

    Oh, how slowly have I often
      Follow'd where Thy hand would draw,
    How Thy kindness fail'd to soften,
      How Thy chastening fail'd to awe.

EVENING:—

Do I deem my griefs not worthy to be compared with heavenly glory?—(*Rom.* viii. 18.)

    Oh! reckon light thine earthly griefs,
      When counterpoised with glory's weight,
    Or balanced with the sweet reliefs
      Oft sent their wo to mitigate.

APRIL 13.

MORNING:—

"I will lay mine hand upon my mouth."—*Job* xl. 4.

> To me, or good or evil send,
> As seemeth best to Thee;
> And teach my stubborn soul to bend
> In love to Thy decree.

NOON:—

"I know that it shall be well with them that fear God, which fear before Him."—*Eccles.* viii. 12.

> Life bringeth me no careless sting;
> Death can but crown my bliss,
> And waft me, on an angel's wing,
> Away to happiness.

EVENING:—

Do I own my griefs lighter than my sins?—(*Job* xi. 6.)

> God will not always chide;
> And when His strokes are felt,
> His strokes are fewer than our crimes,
> And lighter than our guilt.

APRIL 14.

MORNING :—

"God forbid that I should glory, save in the cross of our Lord Jesus Christ."—*Gal.* vi. 14.

> Fruit of the curse, the tangled *thorn*
>   Show'd that He bore its deadly sting;
> The *crown*, 'mid Israel's cruel scorn,
>   Mark'd Him as earth's anointed King.

NOON :—

"Every eye shall see Him, and they also which pierced Him."—*Rev.* i. 7.

> The soldier, as He pierced Thee, proved
>   Man's hatred, Lord, to Thee;
> While, in the blood that stain'd the spear,
>   Love, only love, we see.

EVENING :—

Was not my Saviour's cross heavier than mine?—(*Heb.* xii. 2.)

> I look to Jesus, and the sight
>   Of all that He endured for me,
> Makes e'en my greatest sufferings light,
>   Compared with His deep agony.

APRIL 15.

MORNING :—
"All the days of my appointed time will I wait, till my change come."—*Job* xiv. 14.
Soon wilt Thou take us to Thy tranquil bower,
    To rest one little hour,
Till Thine elect are number'd, and the grave
    Call Thee to come and save.

NOON :—
"They took Him down from the tree, and laid Him in a sepulchre."—*Acts* xiii. 29.
Walk in the light, and e'en the tomb
    No fearful shade shall wear;
Glory shall chase away its gloom,
    'For Christ hath conquer'd there.

EVENING :—
Am I crucified with Christ?—(*Gal.* ii. 20.)
Counting gain and glory loss,
    May I tread the path He trod,
Die with Jesus on the cross,
    Rise with Him to Thee, my God.

APRIL 16.

MORNING :—

"This is the day which the Lord hath made; we will rejoice and be glad in it."—*Psa*. cxviii. 24.

>Sing praise! the tomb is void
> Where the Redeemer lay!
>Sing of our bonds destroy'd,
> Our darkness turn'd to day!

NOON :—

"The Lord is risen indeed."—*Luke* xxiv. 34.

>Not long the toils of hell could keep
> The hope of Judah's line;
>Corruption never could take hold
> On aught so much divine.

EVENING :—

Am I risen with Christ?—(*Col.* iii. 1.)

>Soar we now where Christ hath led,
>Following our exalted Head;
>Made like Him, like Him we rise,
>Our's the cross, the grave, the skies.

APRIL 17.

MORNING:—

"We labour that...we may be accepted of Him."—2 *Cor.* v. 9.

> Oh, by Thy saving power,
>   So make us live and die,
> That we may stand in THAT dread hour
>   At Thy right hand on high.

NOON:—

"Him hath God exalted with His right hand to be a Prince and a Saviour."—*Acts* v. 31.

> Jesus, the gift impart
>   Thy risen power to know;
> And teach each quicken'd heart
>   In Thy true love to glow.

EVENING:—

Do I look for the coming of Christ?—(*Heb.* ix. 28.)

> 'Tis but a little while,
>   And He shall come again,
> Who died that we might live,—who lives
>   That we with Him may reign.

APRIL 18.

Morning:—

"Let us go speedily to pray before the Lord, and to seek the Lord of hosts."—*Zech.* viii. 21.

    Thus many a Bethel shall record
    The promised presence of the Lord;
    And may each home a Bethel prove,
    The dwelling of the God of love.

Noon:—

"He blesseth the habitation of the just."—*Prov.* iii. 33.

    As different scenes of life arise,
      Our grateful hearts would be
    With Thee amid the social band—
      In solitude with Thee.

Evening:—

Do I join with others in holy vow and effort?—(*Eccles.* iv. 9.)

    'Tis sweet to raise the common song,
      To join in holy praise and love,
    And imitate the blessed throng
      That mingle hearts and songs above.

APRIL 19.

MORNING :—

"I will go also."—*Zech.* viii. 21.

Be this the purpose of my soul,
   My solemn, my determined choice,
To yield to His supreme control,
   And in His kind commands rejoice.

NOON :—

"If thou be wise, thou shalt be wise for thyself."—*Prov.* ix. 12.

O Thou source of every blessing,
   Guide a trembling sinner on,
Till in heaven, Thy smile possessing,
   Grace shall be my endless song.

EVENING :—

Do I bear in mind my personal responsibility?—(*Acts* xxvii. 23.)

Oh, make me faithful unto death,
Thy witness with my latest breath,
To tell the glories of the Lamb,—
Him whom I serve, and whose I am.

APRIL 20.

Morning :—

"I will call on the Lord, who is worthy to be praised."—2 *Sam.* xxii. 4.

Praise, Lord, for Thee in Zion waits;
Prayer shall besiege Thy temple gates;
All flesh shall to Thy throne repair,
And find through Christ salvation there.

Noon :—

"The Lord giveth wisdom; out of His mouth cometh knowledge and understanding."—*Prov.* ii. 6.

'Tis ours, to ask and to receive,
  To take, and not to buy;
'Tis Thine in sovereign grace to give,
  Yea, give abundantly.

Evening :—

Do I feel my need of help?—(2 *Tim.* ii. 1.)

Unsustain'd by Thee I fall,
Lend the strength for which I call;
Weaker than a bruised reed,
Help I every moment need.

APRIL 21.

MORNING :—

"Behold, God is my salvation; I will trust, and not be afraid."—*Isa.* xii. 2.

Lodged in Thine arms, I fear no more,
The tempest's howl, the billow's roar;
Those storms must shake the Almighty's seat,
Which violate the saint's retreat.

NOON :—

"Be not wise in thine own eyes."—*Prov.* iii. 7.

The souls that would to Jesus cleave,
    And hear His secret call,
Must their own strength and wisdom leave,
    And let the Lord be all.

EVENING :—

Is it self-trust that hinders my trust in God?—(*Prov.* iii. 5.)

    O Lord, with sorrow I confess
        I have distrusted Thee,
    Yet now bestow the needful grace
        That I may faithful be

APRIL 23.

MORNING :—

"I will not fear what flesh can do unto me."—*Psa.* lvi. 4.

The taunts and frowns of men on earth,
    What are they all to me?
Oh, they are things of little worth,
    Weigh'd with one smile from Thee!

NOON :—

"Without were fightings, and within were fears."—2 *Cor.* vii. 5.

Oh, 'tis uphill work the Christian's life,
    With its fightings without and its fears within,
Yet he would not exchange that holy strife
    For the softest sleep in the paths of sin.

EVENING :—

Is Christ my only and all-sufficient hope?—(1 *Tim.* i. 1.)

    On His great love
    Our hopes we place
    Of present grace
    And joys above.

APRIL 23.

MORNING :—

"I will hope continually."—*Psa.* lxxi. 14.

> Hope in the sunshine basketh
> Of His eternal truth,
> The wondrous plant which bloometh
> In green perpetual youth.

NOON :—

"The fear of the Lord tendeth to life; and he that hath it, shall abide satisfied."—*Prov.* xix. 23.

> When will no thought ever enter
> Into mind and heart but this,
> In the Lord alone to centre
> Every hope of happiness!

EVENING :—

Do I strive to see the bright side of things?—(1 *Pet.* i. 6.)

> What of the night, watchman, what of the
>   Tho' the wintry gales sweep by, [night?
> When the darkest hour begins to lower
>   We know that the dawn is nigh.

APRIL 24.

Morning:—

"Thy word have I hid in mine heart, that I might not sin against Thee."—*Psa.* cxix. 11.

To purify ourselves as He is pure,
  To follow in the path which Jesus trod,
To love, to trust, to hope, and to endure,—
  This is the life acceptable to God.

Noon:—

"Wherefore should I fear in the days of evil?"—*Psa.* xlix. 5.

Weep we may,—rebel we must not,
  Though by thousand cares oppress'd.
Low we're brought, but sink we cannot,
  While we lean on Jesus' breast.

Evening:—

Have I governed my emotions?— (*Phil.* iv. 5.)

I weep, but not rebellious tears;
  I mourn, but not in hopeless wo;
I droop, but not with doubtful fears,
  For whom I've trusted, Him I know.

APRIL 25.

MORNING :—

"I am purposed that my mouth shall not transgress."—*Psa*. xvii. 3.

The tongue, that most unruly power,
　Requires a strong restraint;
We must be watchful every hour,
　And pray, and never faint.

NOON :—

"Death and life are in the power of the tongue."—*Prov*. xviii. 21.

Oh! many a shaft, at random sent,
Finds mark the archer little meant;
And many a word, at random spoken,
May soothe or wound a heart that's broken.

EVENING :—

Have I watched my words and acts? —(1 *Tim*. iv. 12.)

Were Christ's commands before my sight
　In all I thought and spoke?
And have I borne His burden light,
　And worn His easy yoke?

APRIL 26.

MORNING :—

"I have hated the congregation of evil-doers, and will not sit with the wicked."—*Psa.* xxvi. 5.

> From wicked men will I withdraw,
> And sinful ways forsake,
> And only those who love Thy law
> For my companions take.

NOON :—

"Surely He scorneth the scorners."—*Prov.* iii. 34.

> Through the skies when Thy thunder is [hurl'd,
> The child to its parent will flee;
> Thus amidst the rebukes of the world,
> I turn, O my Father, to Thee.

EVENING :—

Have I kept my heart with all diligence?—(*Prov.* iv. 23.)

> By conscience traced, now let me read
> The unflattering records of the day,
> Each thought of sin, each evil deed;
> Alas, how long the dark array!

APRIL 27.

Morning :—

"I will...praise Thy name for Thy lovingkindness and for Thy truth."—*Psa.* cxxxviii. 2.

> In every smiling happy hour,
>   Be this my sweet employ;
> Thy praise refines mine earthly bliss,
>   And doubles all my joy.

Noon :—

"He is a shield unto them that put their trust in Him."—*Prov.* xxx. 5.

> I praise the God of grace,
>   I trust His truth and might;
> He calls me His, I call Him mine,
>   My God, my joy, my light.

Evening :—

Does the name of Christ assure my soul?—(*John* i. 12.)

> It tells me of a Father's smile
>   Beaming upon His child;
> It cheers me through this "little while,"
>   Mid desert, waste, and wild.

APRIL 28.

MORNING:—

"My praise shall be continually of Thee."—*Psa.* lxxi. 6.

> Thy nature, Lord, no change can know;
>   Thy promise still is sure;
> And ills can ne'er so hopeless grow,
>   But Thou canst find a cure.

NOON:—

"The righteous doth sing and rejoice."—*Prov.* xxix. 6.

> Who but a Christian, through all life,
>   That blessing may prolong?
> Who, through the world's sad day of strife,
>   Still chant his matin song?

EVENING:—

Does the name of Christ strengthen my soul?—(*Acts* iii. 16.)

> Dear name! the rock on which I build;
>   My shield and hiding-place;
> My never-failing treasury, fill'd
>   With boundless stores of grace.

APRIL 29.

Morning :—

"I will yet praise Thee more and more."—*Psa.* lxxi. 14.

> My Saviour, my Almighty Friend,
> When I begin Thy praise,
> Where will the growing numbers end,
> The numbers of Thy grace?

Noon :—

"He that soweth iniquity shall reap vanity."—*Prov.* xxii. 8.

> Strange that my soul should cleave to dust,
> With death and heaven so nigh!
> Begone, vain world! my spirit must
> Ascend to dwell on high.

Evening :—

Does the name of Christ refresh my soul?—(*S. Song* i. 3.)

> I love the name of Jesus,
> Emmanuel, Christ the Lord;
> Like fragrance on the breezes
> His name is shed abroad.

APRIL 30.

MORNING :—

"I will behave myself wisely in a perfect way."—*Psa.* ci. 2.

> Perish policy and cunning!
> Perish all that fears the light!
> Whether losing, whether winning,
> Trust in God, and do the right.

NOON :—

"Commit thy works unto the Lord."—*Prov.* xvi. 3.

> .... The wise and true
> Crave not for lofty tasks, but turn the small
> To greatness, by the great heart doing all
> For God ....

EVENING :—

Have I learned to live by the day only?—(*Matt.* vi. 34.)

> What Thou shalt to-day provide,
> Let me as a child receive;
> What to-morrow may betide,
> Calmly to Thy wisdom leave.

MAY 1.

Morning:

"Teach me Thy way, O Lord; I will walk in Thy truth." *Psa.* lxxxvi. 11.

> If God to me His statutes show,
> And heavenly truth impart,
> His work for ever I'll pursue,
> His law shall rule my heart.

Noon:

"Meddle not with them that are given to change."—*Prov.* xxiv. 21.

> Calm, when the great world's news with power
> My listening spirits stir,
> Let not the tidings of the hour
> E'er find TOO fond an ear.

Evening:—

Do I realize a life hid with Christ? —(*Col.* iii. 3.)

> Great is the peace Thy grace bestows
> Mid storms of earthly strife,
> And calm and sweet is their repose
> Who live this hidden life.

MAY 2.

Morning :—

"I will not forget Thy word."—
Psa. cxix. 16.

Teach me, O Lord, to prize Thy word,
   This gift of matchless favour;
Make it my wealth, my joy, my health,
   My strength and life for ever.

Noon :—

"Forget not My law, but let thine heart keep My commandments."—
Prov. iii. 1.

Wouldst thou be wise, and know the Lord?
   Wouldst thou believe aright?
Make the blest volume of His word
   Thy rule, thy guide, thy light.

Evening :—

Is my soul's life fed by the word?—
(1 *Pet.* ii. 2.)

Thy light and truth shall guide me still,
   Thy word shall my best thoughts employ,
And lead me to Thy heavenly hill,
   My God, my most exceeding joy.

MAY 8.

MORNING:—

"I will teach you the good and the right way."—1 *Sam.* xii. 23.

Chief Shepherd of Thy chosen sheep,
From shame and death set free,
May every under-shepherd keep
His eye intent on Thee.

NOON:—

"A word spoken in due season, how good is it?"—*Prov.* xv. 23.

Oh, may our dull and languid zeal
Be kindled to a flame,
And burn till all the earth shall feel
The glories of His name.

EVENING:—

Have I heard the voice which says, "Come"?—(*Rev.* xxii. 17.)

Come hither, bring thy boding fears,
Thine aching heart, thy bursting tears,
'Tis Mercy's voice salutes thine ears;
O trembling sinner, come.

MAY 4.

MORNING:—

"I will pray for you unto the Lord."
—1 *Sam.* vii. 5.

> Many around us blindly stray;
> Moved with pity, let us pray,—
> Pray that those who now are blind
> Soon the way of truth may find.

NOON:—

"By the blessing of the upright the city is exalted."—*Prov.* xi. 11.

> The practised archer's bow may fail,
>   The shield give no defence,
> But prayer is certain to prevail,
>   It moves Omnipotence.

EVENING:—

Do I long to see others brought to Christ?—(*Acts* xxvi. 28, 29.)

> The light that on our souls hath shone
>   Leads us in hope to Thee;
> Let us not feel its rays alone,
>   Alone Thy people be.

MAY 5.

Morning:—

"For Zion's sake will I not hold my peace, and for Jerusalem's sake I will not rest."—*Isa.* lxii. 1.

> Lord, Thou didst love Jerusalem;
> Once she was all Thine own;
> Her love Thy fairest heritage;
> Her power, Thy glory's throne!

Noon:—

"Where the word of a king is, there is power."—*Eccles.* viii. 4.

> Mighty to vanquish and forgive!
> Thine Israel shall repent and live,
> And loud proclaim Thy healing breath
> Which works their life who wrought Thy death.

Evening:—

Do I pray for the peace of Jerusalem?—(*Psa.* cxxii. 6.)

> Come shall the day, and come it may full soon,
> When thou, more splendid than the moon,
> Shalt rise, and triumphing o'er night,
> Turn ebon darkness into silver light.

MAY 6.

MORNING :—
"I long to see you, that I may impart unto you some spiritual gift."—*Rom.* i. 11.

May He by whose kind care we meet,
   Send His good Spirit from above,
Make our communications sweet,
   And cause our hearts to burn with love.

NOON :—
"Iron sharpeneth iron; so a man sharpeneth the countenance of his friend."—*Prov.* xxvii. 17.

Great the joy when Christians meet!
Christian fellowship, how sweet,
When, their theme of praise the same,
They exalt Jehovah's name.

EVENING :—
Do I value the fellowship of saints?—(2 *Cor.* vii. 13.)

   Bind Thy people, Lord, in union,
     With the sevenfold cord of love:
   Breathe a spirit of communion
     With the glorious hosts above.

MAY 7.

MORNING :—

"My mouth shall speak of wisdom."
—*Psa.* xlix. 3.

> Wisdom has treasures greater far
>   Than East and West unfold,
> And her rewards more precious are
>   Than is the gain of gold.

NOON :—

"My fruit is better than gold, yea, than fine gold."—*Prov.* viii. 19.

> Though our lot be crown'd with blessing,
>   Bless'd in basket and in store,
> Every earthly gift possessing,
>   All—save Jesus,—we are poor.

EVENING :—

Do I prize communion with God above all else?—(*John* xvi. 32.)

> Tho' our path seem dark and lonely;
>   Reft of glory;—poor and sad;—
> Friends estranged;—with Jesus only,
>   We are rich, and full, and glad.

MAY 8.

MORNING:—

"Go, work to-day in my vineyard... And he said, I GO, sir."—*Matt.* xxi. 28, 30.

> The vineyard of their Lord
> Before His labourers lies;
> And, lo! we see the vast reward
> Which waits us in the skies.

NOON:—

"He said, I go, sir; and went NOT."—*Matt.* xxi. 30.

> Why is my heart so far from Thee,
> My God, my chief delight?
> Why are my thoughts no more by day
> With Thee,—no more by night?

EVENING:—

Do I look for higher communion above?—(*John* xvii. 22—24.)

> A few more Sabbaths here
> Shall cheer us on our way,
> And we shall reach the blissful rest,
> The eternal Sabbath-day.

MAY 9.

MORNING:—

"I will not be negligent to put you in remembrance."—2 *Pet.* i. 12, *comp.* 14.

> Beyond the smiling and the weeping,
> Beyond the waking and the sleeping,
> Beyond the sowing and the reaping,
>   I shall be soon.

NOON:—

"Happy is the man that findeth wisdom."—*Prov.* iii. 13.

> Once the world was all my treasure,
>   Then the world my heart possess'd;
> Now I taste sublimer pleasure,
>   Since the Lord has made me blest.

EVENING:—

Do I employ my time for Christ?— (*Col.* iv. 5.)

> What have I done for Him that died
>   To save my wretched soul?
> How are my follies multiplied,
>   Fast as my minutes roll!

MAY 10.

MORNING:—

"From henceforth I will go unto the Gentiles."—*Acts* xviii. 6.

> Who are ready now to sever
> Bands that round their hearts entwine?
> Who will go, resolving never
> Under sufferings to repine?

NOON:—

"To him that soweth righteousness shall be a sure reward."—*Prov.* xi. 18.

> Lord, grant us all divine success
> Amidst our arduous toil;
> The seed shall have a large increase,
> If Thou prepare the soil.

EVENING:—

Can I deny myself for Christ's sake?—(*John* iv. 34.)

> Thy bright example I'd pursue,
> To Thee in all things rise;
> Let all I think, or speak, or do,
> Be one great sacrifice.

MAY 11.

MORNING :—

"I am ready...to die...for the name of the Lord Jesus."—*Acts* xxi. 13.

> My friendship's utmost zeal to try,
> He asked if I for Him would die?
> The flesh was weak, my blood ran chill,
> But the free spirit cried, "I will."

NOON :—

"The Lord trieth the hearts."—*Prov.* xvii. 3.

> Let me be with Thee where Thou art,
>   Where spotless saints Thy name adore;
> Then only will this sinful heart
>   Be evil and defiled no more.

EVENING :—

Can I bear reproach for Christ?—(*Acts* v. 41.)

> Show me the cross that I must bear;
>   Bend my proud heart, that I may take
> In holy faith and humble prayer
>   The cross of shame for Thy dear sake.

MAY 19.

MORNING:—

"At Thy word I will let down the net."—*Luke* v. 5.

Upon the Lord thou must rely,
  If thou wouldst win success;
Upon His work must fix thine eye,
  Ere He thy work can bless.

NOON:—

"The lips of the righteous feed many."—*Prov.* x. 21.

Thy gifts are only then enjoy'd
  When used as talents lent,—
Those talents only well employ'd
  When in Thy service spent.

EVENING:—

Would unbroken success be good for me?—(2 *Cor.* xii. 7.)

God will not let Love's work impart
Full solace, lest it steal the heart;
Be thou content in tears to sow,
Blessing, like Jesus, in thy wo.

MAY 13.

MORNING:—

"I will praise Thee among much people."—*Psa.* xxxv. 18.

> Bid the whole earth, responsive now
>   To the bright world above,
> Break forth in sweetest strains of joy,
>   In memory of Thy love.

NOON:—

"The time of the singing of birds is come."—*S. Song* ii. 12.

> And shall the first beloved of heaven
>   Mute listen as they sing?
> Shall man, to whom the lyre is given,
>   Not wake one tuneful string?

EVENING:—

Why am I so lukewarm in praise? —(*Lam.* v. 15—17.)

> To other strains our souls are set,—
>   A giddy whirl of sin
> Fills ear and brain, and will not let
>   Heaven's harmonies come in.

MAY 14.

MORNING:—

"I will show forth all Thy marvellous works."—*Psa.* ix. 1.

Salvation! oh, salvation!
The joyful sound proclaim,
Till each remotest nation
Has learn'd Messiah's name.

NOON:—

"He that followeth after righteousness and mercy, findeth life."—*Prov.* xxi. 21.

Kept peaceful in the midst of strife,
Forgiving and forgiven,
Oh, may we lead the pilgrim's life,
And follow Thee to heaven.

EVENING:—

Where are the souls I have sought to bless?—(2 *Cor.* v. 11.)

Day by day, and hour by hour,
Serve the Lord with all your power;
Though your talent be but small,
He who gave it claims it all.

MAY 15.

MORNING:—

"I will judge uprightly."—*Psa.* lxxv. 2.

>Oh, purge my vision, Lord,
>   That I may truth discern,
>And, all things proving by Thy word,
>   From all things sinful turn.

NOON:—

"Every way of a man is right in his own eyes."—*Prov.* xxi. 2.

>Judge not hastily of others,
>   But thine own salvation mind,
>Nor be lynx-eyed to thy brother's—
>   To thine own offences, blind.

EVENING:—

Am I impartial in my judgments.—(*John* vii. 24.)

>Have I the widow's plaint contemn'd?
>   Have I despised the orphan's prayer?
>Have I the righteous cause condemned?
>   Or sought the sordid bribe to share?

MAY 16.

MORNING:—

"Fear ye not; I will nourish you and your little ones."—*Gen.* l. 21.

 The widow's heart shall sing for joy,
  The orphan shall be fed,
 And hungering souls we'll gladly point
  To Christ, the living Bread.

NOON:—

"The merciful man doeth good to his own soul."—*Prov.* xi. 17.

 Grant that our souls, renew'd by Thee,
 In faith and friendship may agree,
 And for Thy sake delight to heal,
 Or share the pain which others feel.

EVENING:—

Am I charitable as well as just?—(2 *Pet.* i. 7.)

 If I have turn'd away
From grief or suffering which I might relieve,
Careless the cup of water e'en to give,
 Now pardon, Lord, I pray.

MAY 17.

MORNING:—

"Let the righteous smite me; it shall be a kindness."—*Psa.* cxli. 5.

Oh, may the righteous, when I stray,
Smite and reprove my wandering way;
Their gentle words, like ointment shed,
Shall never bruise, but cheer my head.

NOON:—

"Meddle not with him that flattereth with his lips."—*Prov.* xx. 19.

When men exalt thee with their flatteries,
Be thou provoked thine own self to despise,
And, for an help to this, the meanest thing
Which thou hast ever done, to memory bring.

EVENING:—

Am I humble as well as charitable?—(1 *Pet.* v. 5.)

Is not haughtiness of heart
   The gulf between my God and me?
Meek Redeemer, now impart
   Thine own humility.

MAY 18.

MORNING:—

"I would seek unto God."—*Job* v. 8.

> O Father, compass me about
>   With love, for I am weak;
> Forgive, forgive each sinful doubt,
>   For unto Thee I seek.

NOON:—

"There shall no evil happen to the just."—*Prov.* xii. 21.

> My lifted eye, without one tear,
>   The gathering storm shall see;
> My trembling heart shall own no fear
>   While it can trust in Thee.

EVENING:—

I am afflicted; do I pray?—(*James* v. 13.)

> The heart sustain'd by Christ, though deep
>   Its anguish, still can bear;
> The soul He condescends to keep,
>   Shall never know despair.

MAY 19.

Morning :—

"I will cry unto God most High, unto God that performeth all things for me."—*Psa.* lvii. 2.

> True faith applies vast Providence
>   To each peculiar grief and groan;
> Yea, grasps believ'd Omnipotence,
>   As though it ruled for her alone.

Noon :—

"By sadness...the heart is made better."—*Eccles.* vii. 3.

> If vex'd with grief, distress, and pain,
>   A Father strikes the blow;
> In every trouble there is gain,—
>   On every cloud a bow.

Evening :—

Do I value the privilege of prayer? —(*Phil.* iv. 6.)

> I love to walk with Jesus,
>   To lean upon His breast,
> And hear Him sweetly whisper
>   "I, I will give thee rest."

MAY 20.

MORNING:—

"Because He hath inclined His ear unto me, therefore will I call upon Him as long as I live."—*Psa.* cxvi. 2.

> In the hour of sore affliction
>   God hath seen and pitied thee;
> Cheer thee in the sweet conviction,
>   Thou henceforth His care shalt be.

NOON:—

"He that walketh in his uprightness feareth the Lord."—*Prov.* xiv. 2.

> Midst hourly cares, may love present
>   Its incense to Thy throne;
> And while the world our hands employs,
>   Our hearts be Thine alone.

EVENING:—

Do my prayers aim beyond the supply of my own wants?—(*Hos.* vii. 14.)

> Prayer was not meant for luxury,
>   Or selfish pastime sweet;
> It is the prostrate creature's place
>   At his Creator's feet.

MAY 21.

MORNING:—

"I have taken upon me to speak unto the Lord."—*Gen.* xviii. 27.

The prayers I make will then be sweet indeed,
  If Thou the Spirit give, by which I pray:
  My unassisted heart is barren clay,
That of its native self can nothing feed.

NOON:—

"His children shall have a place of refuge."—*Prov.* xiv. 26.

    Enough, my gracious Lord,
      Let faith triumphant cry;
    My heart can on this promise live,
      Can on this promise die.

EVENING:—

Are mine the idle prayers of the formalist?—(*Isa.* xxix. 13.)

  Not words alone it cost the Lord
    To purchase pardon for His own;
  Nor will a soul, by grace restored,
    Return the Saviour words alone.

MAY 22.

MORNING:—

"If I forget thee, O Jerusalem, let my right hand forget her cunning."—*Psa.* cxxxvii. 5, 6.

> Oh, let my hand forget her skill,
> My tongue be silent, cold, and still,
> This bounding heart forget to beat,
> If I forget the Mercy-seat.

NOON:—

"He that diligently seeketh good procureth favour."—*Prov.* xi. 27.

> Why should this anxious load
>   Press down your weary mind?
> Haste to your heavenly Father's throne,
>   And sweet refreshment find.

EVENING:—

Are mine the proud prayers of the self-righteous?—(*Luke* xviii. 11—14.)

> Mercy alone can meet my case;
>   For mercy, Lord, I cry;
> Jesus, Redeemer, show Thy face
>   In mercy, or I die.

MAY 23.

MORNING:—

"Our feet shall stand within thy gates, O Jerusalem."—*Psa.* cxxii. 2.

> I love her gates, I love the road;
> The church, adorn'd with grace,
> Stands like a palace built for God,
> To show His milder face.

NOON:—

"I will pour upon [them] the Spirit of grace and of supplications."—*Zech.* xii. 10.

> When the fervent prayer is glowing,
> Holy Spirit, hear that prayer;
> When the song of praise is flowing,
> Let that song Thine impress bear.

EVENING:—

Are mine the vain prayers of the Pharisee?—(*Matt.* vi. 5, 6.)

> I come to Thee to-night,
> In my lone closet where no eye can see,
> And dare to crave an interview with Thee,
> Father of love and light!

MAY 24.

Morning:—

"Thou hast been a shelter for me; ...I will trust in the covert of Thy wings."—*Psa.* lxi. 3, 4.

 Contented, cheerful, may I learn,
  To trust Thy care divine;
 As providence is Thy concern,
  Be resignation mine.

Noon:—

"Whoso putteth his trust in the Lord shall be safe."—*Prov.* xxix. 25.

All my trust on Thee is stay'd;
 All my help from Thee I bring;
Cover my defenceless head
 With the shadow of Thy wing.

Evening:—

Is Christ able and willing to shelter me?—(*Matt.* xxiii. 37.)

How oft beneath His blest and healing wings
He would have gather'd me, and I would not;
Like a weak bird, all heedless of my lot,
 Perverse and idle in my wanderings.

MAY 25.

MORNING:—

"What time I am afraid, I will trust in Thee."—*Psa.* lvi. 3.

> His arms of love enclosing
>   The weary and distress'd,
> They, on His heart reposing,
>   Shall find a blissful rest.

NOON:—

"The name of the Lord is a strong tower; the righteous runneth into it, and is safe."—*Prov.* xviii. 10.

> Bulwarks of mighty grace defend
>   The city where we dwell;
> The walls, of strong salvation made,
>   Defy the assaults of hell.

EVENING:—

Is not the King of kings stronger than the king of terrors? (1 *Cor.* xv. 57.)

> For saints, invert no emblem torch,
>   As though death won the strife;
> To die is but to gain the porch
>   Of endless, griefless life.

MAY 26.

MORNING:—

"In God have I put my trust; I will not be afraid what man can do unto me."—*Psa.* lvi. 11.

> If God be my Salvation,
>   My Refuge in distress,
> What earthly tribulation
>   Can shake my inward peace?

NOON:—

"The fear of man bringeth a snare."
—*Prov.* xxix. 25.

> Faith lifts the veil, and makes it clear,
>   In all the times of pain and grief,
> No harm is nigh us but from fear,
>   No danger save from unbelief.

EVENING:—

Has the fear of God cast out every other fear?—(*Luke* xii. 4, 5.)

> Lord, let Thy fear within us dwell,
>   Thy love our footsteps guide;
> Thy love shall all vain love expel,
>   Thy fear all fear beside.

MAY 27.

MORNING :—

"I will praise the Lord according to His righteousness."—*Psa.* vii. 17.

> Sweet is the memory of Thy grace,
>   My God, my heavenly King;
> Let age to age Thy righteousness
>   In sounds of glory sing.

NOON :—

"Hast thou not known Me?...he that hath seen Me hath seen the Father."—*John* xiv. 9.

> With justice, mercy, truth replete,
> How sweetly Thy perfections meet,
> Concentred in Immanuel's face,
> Blest image of His Father's grace.

EVENING :—

Do I realize the nearness of God? —(*Psa.* xvi. 8.)

> Until the crown is given,
>   And I with Thee appear,
> Be this my constant heaven
>   To feel Thy presence here.

MAY 28.

MORNING:—

"I will...ascribe righteousness to my Maker."—*Job* xxxvi. 3.

> He everywhere hath sway,
>   And all things serve His might;
> His every act pure blessing is;
>   His path, unsullied light.

NOON:—

"Come unto Me, all ye that labour and are heavy laden, and I will give you rest."—*Matt.* xi. 28.

> He to thine every trial knows
>   Its just restraint to give,
> Attentive to behold thy woes,
>   And faithful to relieve.

EVENING:—

Do I patiently wait God's time?—(*Heb.* x. 36.)

> He knows how long the wilful heart
>   Requires the chastening grief;
> And soon as sorrow's work is done,
>   'Tis He who sends relief.

MAY 29.

MORNING :—

"My tongue also shall talk of Thy righteousness."—*Psa.* lxxi. 24.

> Let not my tongue alone proclaim
>   The honours of my God;
> My life, with all its active powers,
>   Shall spread Thy praise abroad.

NOON :—

"Ye shall find rest unto your souls."—*Matt.* xi. 29.

> Be still, my soul, let nothing stir
>   Thee from the sweet repose
> Of those who to their God refer
>   Their joys, their cares, their woes.

EVENING :—

Am I convinced that in all things God is Love?—(*Rev.* iii. 19.)

> We cannot always trace the way,
>   When Thou, our gracious Lord, dost move;
> But we can always surely say
>   That Thou art Love.

MAY 30.

MORNING :—

"I will keep Thy statutes.; O forsake me not utterly."—*Psa.* cxix. 8.

  Oh, hide this self from me, that I
    No more, but Christ in me, may live ;
  My vile affections crucify,
    Nor let one darling lust survive.

NOON :—

"If sinners entice thee, consent thou not."—*Prov.* i. 10.

    I ask a sober mind,
      A self-renouncing will,
    That tramples down and casts behind
      The baits of pleasing ill.

EVENING :—

Am I set apart as king and priest to God?—(1 *Pet.* ii. 9.)

    'Tis His love His people raises
      Over self to reign as kings;
    And, as priests, His solemn praises
      Each for a thank-offering brings.

MAY 31.

MORNING:—

"I will set no wicked thing before mine eyes."—*Psa.* ci. 3.

O Lord, with strength my soul endue;
My purpose fix; my heart renew;
Thine all-transforming grace inspire,
And grant me my supreme desire.

NOON:—

"The hearing ear, and the seeing eye, the Lord hath made even both of them."—*Prov.* xx. 12.

From worldly strife, from mirth unblest,
Drowning Thy music in the breast,
From foul reproach, from thrilling fears,
Preserve, good Lord, Thy servant's ears.

EVENING:—

Do I aspire after heavenly purity?—(*Rev.* xiv. 5.)

Oh for a heart that never sins;
Oh for a soul wash'd white;
Oh for a voice to praise our King,
Nor weary day or night!

JUNE 1.

MORNING :—

"I will take heed that I sin not with my tongue."—*Psa.* xxxix. 1.

> May our lips, from sin set free,
> Love to speak and sing of Thee,
> Till in heaven we learn to raise
> Hymns of everlasting praise.

NOON :—

"The simple believeth every word; but the prudent man looketh well to his going."—*Prov.* xiv. 15.

> Be Thou my guard on peril's brink,
>   Be Thou my guide through weal or wo,
> And teach me of Thy cup to drink,
>   And make me in Thy path to go.

EVENING :—

Do I in the desert taste of Canaan's fruit?—(*Numb.* xiii. 23.)

> The men of grace have found
>   Glory begun below;
> Celestial fruits on earthly ground
>   From faith and hope may grow.

JUNE 2.

MORNING :—

"Every day will I bless Thee."—*Psa.* cxlv. 2.

> For ever let my grateful heart
> His boundless grace adore,
> Who gives ten thousand blessings now,
> And bids me hope for more.

NOON :—

"Whilst we are at home in the body, we are absent from the Lord."—2 *Cor.* v. 6.

> Prepare us, Lord, by grace divine,
> For Thy bright courts on high,
> Then bid our spirits rise and join
> The chorus of the sky.

EVENING :—

Do I repose on a Father's care?—(*Psa.* ciii. 13.)

> Thou art as much His care as if beside
> Nor man nor angel lived in heaven or earth;
> Thus sunbeams pour alike their glorious tide
> To light up worlds, or wake an insect's mirth.

JUNE 8.

Morning:—

"I will praise Thy name, O Lord; for it is good."—*Psa.* liv. 6.

> To God the Father, God the Son,
> And God the Spirit, Three in One,
> Be honour, praise, and glory given,
> By all on earth, and all in heaven.

Noon:—

"God is with us."—*Isa.* viii. 10.

> Near us, when in doubt, to guide us;
> Near us, when we faint, to cheer;
> Near, in battle's hour, to hide us;
> Nearer ever, and more dear.

Evening:—

Do I rest implicitly and thankfully on the Saviour's fully finished work of atonement?—(*Rom.* v. 8—11.)

> May I still enjoy this feeling,
> In all need to Jesus go,
> Prove His wounds each day more healing,
> And Himself more fully know.

JUNE 4.

MORNING:—

"The Lord was ready to save me; therefore we will sing." *Isa.* xxxviii. 20.

All glory to Thy wondrous name,
　Father of mercy, God of love!
Thus we exalt the Lord, the Lamb!
　And thus we praise the heavenly Dove

NOON:—

"When the Comforter is come, whom I will send unto you,...He shall testify of Me."—*John* xv. 26.

Cheer our desponding hearts,
　Thou heavenly Paraclete!
Give us to lie with humble hope
　At our Redeemer's feet.

EVENING:—

Do I seek the baptism of the Holy Ghost?—(*Matt.* iii. 11.)

Come, Holy Spirit, and reveal
　The Son of God to me;
THY powerful influence let me feel,
　And all HIS glories see.

JUNE 5.

Morning :—

"Unto Thee will I pray." *Psa.* v. 2.

See, I am low; yea, very low; but Thou
   Art high, and Thou canst lift me up to Thee;
   *   *   *   *
I am an emptiness for Thee to fill;
   My soul a cavern for Thy sea.

Noon :—

"The Lord will not suffer the soul of the righteous to famish." *Prov.* x. 3.

   My thirsting soul with strong desires
   To God, the living God, aspires;
   Come, gracious Lord, and let me know
   The joys which from Thy presence flow.

Evening :—

Do I expect an answer to my prayers?—(1 *John* v. 14, 15.)

   Depend on Him,—thou canst not fail;
   Make all thy wants and wishes known;
   Fear not; His merits must prevail;
   Ask what thou wilt, it shall be done.

JUNE 6.

MORNING :—

"One thing have I desired of the Lord, that will I seek after; that I may dwell in the house of the Lord."—*Psa.* xxvii. 4.

> We would not live by bread alone,
>   But by Thy word of grace,
> In strength of which we travel on
>   To our abiding-place.

NOON :—

"The spirit shall return unto God who gave it."—*Eccles.* xii. 7.

> This prison where thou art,
>   Thy God will break it soon,
> And flood with light thy heart
>   In His own blessed noon.

EVENING :—

Could I be satisfied to live here for ever?—(*Job* vii. 16.)

> O happy hour when all the storms
>   Of earth shall silent be,
> And our glad souls beyond these stars
>   Shall mount, O Lord, to Thee.

JUNE 7.

MORNING :—

"I will not let Thee go, except Thou bless me."—*Gen.* xxxii. 26.

I will not let Thee go: I'll not forsake my bliss;
  No ;—Thou art mine,
  And I am Thine ;
Thee will I hold, when all things else I miss!

NOON :—

"Lord, help me."—*Matt.* xv. 25.

Till Thou the Father's love reveal,
  Till Thou Thyself bestow,
Be this the cry of every heart,
  "I will not let Thee go."

EVENING :—

Can my soul be content, either in life or death, without God's manifested favour?—(*Psa.* li. 11.)

What were life by Thee ungladden'd
  But a long protracted death ?—
What without Thee would be dying ?
  Night without the morning's breath.

JUNE 10.

MORNING :—

"In the shadow of Thy wings will I make my refuge, until these calamities be overpast."—*Psa*. lvii. 1.

> God is my strong salvation ;
> Then what have I to fear ?
> In darkness and temptation,
> My Light, my Help, is near.

NOON :—

"The fear of the Lord is a fountain of life."—*Prov*. xiv. 27.

> Let my soul, beneath her load,
> Faint not through the o'erwearied flesh ;
> Let her hourly drink afresh
> Love and peace from Thee, my God.

EVENING :—

Where is it that I find unfailing shelter and help ?—(*Psa*. xci. 9, 10.)

> There is an Arm that never tires
> When human strength gives way ;
> There is a love that never fails
> When earthly loves decay.

JUNE 9.

Morning:—

"I cry unto Thee daily."—*Psa.* lxxxvi. 3.

On Thee each morning, O my God,
　My waking thoughts attend;
In Thee are founded all my hopes,
　In Thee my wishes end.

Noon:—

"A wise man feareth, and departeth from evil; but the fool rageth, and is confident."—*Prov.* xiv. 16.

Quick as the apple of the eye,
　O God, my conscience make,
Awake my soul when sin is nigh,
　And keep it still awake.

Evening:—

What is it that most mars my peace?—(*Psa.* xl. 12.)

Had I a throne above the rest,
　Where angels and archangels dwell,
One sin unslain within my breast
　Would make that heaven as dark as hell.

JUNE 12.

Morning:—

"I will declare Thy name unto my brethren."—*Psa.* xxii. 22.

> Build we each the other up;
>   Pray we for our faith's increase,
> Solid comfort, settled hope,
>   Constant joy, and lasting peace.

Noon:—

"We took sweet counsel together, and walked unto the house of God in company."—*Psa.* lv. 14.

> And if our fellowship below
>   In Jesus is so sweet,
> What heights of rapture shall we know
>   When round His throne we meet!

Evening:—

I am nearer heaven; am I fitter for it?—(*Col.* i. 12.)

> Another fleeting day is gone,
>   But soon a fairer day shall rise,—
> A day whose never-setting sun
>   Shall pour its light o'er cloudless skies.

JUNE 13.

MORNING :—

"I will abide in Thy tabernacle for ever."—*Psa*. lxi. 4.

    With water from the smitten rock
      Our thirsty spirits cheer,
    And make us all rejoice to feel
      Thy blessed presence here.

NOON :—

"Whither I go thou canst not follow Me NOW ; but thou shalt follow Me afterwards."—*John* xiii. 36.

    Back to the world ! ah, wo is me,
    In Kedar's tents constrained to be,—
    To dwell with Mesech, when my heart
    Pants to be with Thee where Thou art.

EVENING :—

Life is uncertain : am I prepared to die ?—(*Rom*. xiv. 8.)

    Oh ! may I live with Jesus nigh,
    And sleep in Jesus when I die ;
    Then joyful, when from death I wake,
    I shall eternal bliss partake.

JUNE 14.

MORNING:—

"I will confess my transgressions unto the Lord."—*Psa.* xxxii. 5.

Guilty I stand before Thy face;
  On me I feel Thy wrath abide;
'Tis just the sentence should have place;
  'Tis just;—but, oh! Thy Son hath died.

NOON:—

"Whoso confesseth [his sins] and forsaketh them shall have mercy."—*Prov.* xxviii. 13.

The wounded and the weak
  He comforts, heals, and binds;
The lost He came from heaven to seek,
  And saves them when He finds.

EVENING:—

Do mercies or trials most abound?—(*Gen.* xxxii. 10.)

The way by which a gracious God
  Has led me all my days,
Demands on each review a song
  Of wonder and of praise.

JUNE 15.

MORNING :—

"What have I to do any more with idols?"—*Hos.* xiv. 8.

> Now from the world's vile slavery,
> Almighty Saviour, set me free;
> And, as my treasure is above,
> Be there my thoughts, be there my love.

NOON :—

"There be many things that increase vanity."—*Eccles.* vi. 11.

> Lord, draw my best affections hence,
> Above this world of sin and sense;
> Cause them to soar beyond the skies,
> And rest not till to Thee they rise.

EVENING :—

Does the creature or the Creator fill the throne of my heart?—(1 *John* ii. 16.)

> If I this day have striven
> With Thy blest Spirit, or have bow'd the [knee
> To aught of earth in weak idolatry,
> I pray to be forgiven.

JUNE 16.

MORNING :—

"I will say unto God,...Show me wherefore Thou contendest with me."
—*Job* x. 2.

> On the cross the mystic writing
> Now reveal'd before me lies,
> And I read the words of comfort,
> "As a father I chastise."

NOON :—

"Hear ye the rod, and who hath appointed it."—*Mic.* vi. 9.

> I know whate'er seems good to Thee,
> Is safest, wisest, best for me;
> Oh! teach me, then, to kiss the rod,
> And nearer draw to Thee, my God.

EVENING :—

Does sin or sorrow grieve me most?
—(*Isa.* xxvii. 9.)

> More than for ease in mortal pain,
>   For purity I pray;
> Whatever trials may remain,
>   Oh, take my sins away.

JUNE 17.

MORNING:—

"Come, and let us return unto the Lord."—*Hos.* vi. 1.

> Return, ye wandering souls, return,
>   And seek His tender breast;
> Call back the memory of the days
>   When there you found your rest.

NOON:—

"He shall come unto us as the rain, as the latter and former rain unto the earth."—*Hos.* vi. 3.

> As rain on meadows newly mown,
> So shall He send His influence down;
> His grace on fainting souls distils,
> Like heavenly dew on thirsty hills.

EVENING:—

Have I evidently been with Jesus? —(*Acts* iv. 13.)

> The dew of heaven is like Thy grace;
>   It steals in silence down;
> But where it lights, the favour'd place
>   By richest fruits is known.

JUNE 18.

MORNING :—

"Deliver us out of the hand of our enemies, and we will serve Thee."—1 *Sam.* xii. 10.

> Fear not, though many should oppose;
> Thy God is stronger than thy foes;
> The promised land before thee lies:
> Go, and possess the glorious prize.

NOON :—

"Mercy and truth shall be to them that devise good."—*Prov.* xiv. 22.

> Though kings and nations in His view
>   Are but as motes and dust,
> His eyes and ears are fixed on you
>   Who in His mercy trust.

EVENING :—

Do my sins struggle for mastery?—(*Deut.* xxxiii. 27.)

> He, when old vanquish'd sins arise
>   To rob thee of thy joy,
> Will thrust them forth before thine eyes,
>   And say, "Destroy, destroy!"

JUNE 19.

MORNING:—

"Through Thee will we push down our enemies."—*Psa.* xliv. 5.

> Take courage, and be strong;
> We are passing on to heaven;
> Strength for warfare will be given,
> And glory won ere long.

NOON:—

"The Lord will plead their cause."—*Prov.* xxii. 23.

> Still when danger shall betide us,
> Be Thy warning whisper heard;
> Keep us at Thy feet, and guide us
> By Thy Spirit and Thy word.

EVENING:—

Do I look to Christ for all I need?—(1 *Cor.* i. 30.)

> There as our great High Priest He stands,
> And pleads before the mercy-seat;
> Our cause is in His faithful hands,—
> Our enemies beneath His feet.

JUNE 20.

MORNING:—

"Say NOT thou, I will recompense evil."—*Prov.* xx. 22.

Forgive thy foes; nor that alone,—
  Their evil deeds with good repay;
Fill those with joy who leave thee none,
  And kiss the hand uprais'd to slay.

NOON:—

"Wait on the Lord, and He shall save thee."—*Ibid.*

How fearless should our trust
  In Thy compassion be,
When from our brother of the dust
  We dare appeal to Thee!

EVENING:—

Do I end this day at peace with all around me?—(*Eph.* iv. 26.)

Forgive me, Lord, for Thy dear Son,
The ill that I this day have done;
That with the world, myself, and Thee,
I, ere I sleep, at peace may be.

JUNE 21.

MORNING :—

"I have hated them that regard lying vanities; but I trust in the Lord."—*Psa.* xxxi. 6.

> Joy is a fruit that will not grow
>   In nature's barren soil;
> All we can boast till Christ we know,
>   Is vanity and toil.

NOON :—

"A good man shall be satisfied from himself."—*Prov.* xiv. 14.

> Come, smiling hope, and joy sincere,
> Come, make your constant dwelling here;
> Still let your presence cheer my heart,
> Nor sin compel you to depart.

EVENING :—

Do I end this day at peace with conscience?—(*Gen.* iii. 8.)

> It is the hour when trembling man
>   The voice of heavenly justice heard;
> In wrath the awful tones began,
>   But closed in mercy's whisper'd word.

JUNE 22.

MORNING :—

"My soul followeth hard after Thee."—*Psa.* lxiii. 8.

> To Thee I still would cleave,
>   With ever-growing zeal;
> Let millions tempt me Christ to leave,
>   They never shall prevail.

NOON :—

"He becometh poor that dealeth with a slack hand; but the hand of the diligent maketh rich."—*Prov.* x. 4.

> Forth in Thy name, O Lord, I go
>   My daily labour to pursue,
> Thee, only Thee, resolv'd to know
>   In all I think, or speak, or do.

EVENING :—

Do I end this day at peace with God?—(*Psa.* iv. 8.)

> Lord, how secure and bless'd are they
>   Who feel the joys of pardon'd sin;
> Should storms of wrath shake earth and sea,
>   Their minds have heaven and peace within.

JUNE 23.

MORNING:—

"I will arise and go to my Father."
—*Luke* xv. 18.

> Stranger long to Thee and rest,
>   See the prodigal is come;
> Open wide Thine arms and breast,
>   Take the weary wanderer home.

NOON:—

"He that hardeneth his heart shall fall into mischief."—*Prov.* xxviii. 14.

> Guilty, but with heart relenting,
>   Overwhelm'd with helpless grief,
> Prostrate at Thy feet repenting,
>   Send, oh! send me quick relief.

EVENING:—

Have I been justified by faith?—(*Rom.* v. 1.)

> Jesus, how glorious is Thy grace!
>   When in Thy name we trust,
> Our faith receives a righteousness
>   Which makes the sinner just.

JUNE 24.

MORNING :—

"The meditation of my heart shall be of understanding."—*Psa.* xlix. 3.

> To meditate Thy precepts, Lord,
>   Shall be my sweet employ;
> My soul shall ne'er forget Thy word,
>   Thy word is all my joy.

NOON :—

"Be thou in the fear of the Lord all the day long."—*Prov.* xxiii. 17.

> All day I hear resounding,
>   A voice with silver tone,
> Which speaks of grace abounding
>   Through God's eternal Son.

EVENING :—

Am I standing by faith ? (2 *Cor.* i. 24.)

> O Thou, the contrite sinner's Friend,
>   Who, loving, lovest to the end,
> On this alone my hopes depend,
>   That Thou wilt plead for me.

JUNE 25.

Morning:—

"Draw me; we will run after Thee."—*S. Song* i. 4.

> I need the influence of Thy grace,
>   To speed me in Thy way,
> Lest I should loiter in my race,
>   Or turn my feet astray.

Noon:—

"I drew them with cords of a man, with bands of love."—*Hos.* xi. 4.

> My God, what silken cords are Thine,
>   How soft and yet how strong,
> While power, and truth, and love combine,
>   To draw our souls to Thee!

Evening:—

Is my faith manifest by my works?—(*James* ii. 26.)

> Faith must obey her Father's will,
>   As well as trust His grace;
> A pardoning God is jealous still
>   For His own holiness.

JUNE 26.

MORNING :—

"I myself will awake early."—*Psa.* lvii. 8.

> Awake, my soul, and with the sun
> Thy daily course of duty run;
> Shall off dull sloth, and early rise,
> To pay thy morning sacrifice.

NOON :—

"How long wilt thou sleep, O sluggard? when wilt thou arise out of thy sleep?"—*Prov.* vi. 9.

> Pierce these mists that blind thee;
>   Press to yonder prize;
> Break the bonds that bind thee;
>   Rise, my soul, arise.

EVENING:

What do I possess if I am Christ's? —(1 *Cor.* iii. 21—23.)

> A Hand almighty to defend;
>   An Ear for every call;—
> An honour'd life, a peaceful end,
>   And heaven to crown it all.

JUNE 27.

MORNING :—

"In the morning will I direct my prayer unto Thee, and will look up."
—*Psa.* v. 3.

Teach me Thy love to know,
That this new light, which now I see,
 May both the work and Workman show;
Then by a sunbeam I will climb to Thee.

NOON :—

"He that loveth silver shall not be satisfied with silver."—*Eccles.* v. 10.

Oh! see, in all this noon-tide heat,
How worldlings labour for the meat
That perishes, and comes to nought,
Like shadow when we think 'tis caught.

EVENING :—

Need worldly care hold my eyes waking?—(*Psa.* cxxvii. 2.)

May we, with calm and sweet repose
 And heavenly thoughts refresh'd,
Our eyelids with the morn unclose,
 And bless the Ever-bless'd.

JUNE 28.

MORNING:—

"I will look again toward Thy holy temple."—*Jonah* ii. 4.

.... Thyself reveal ;—
Yet softly !—As the morning glories steal,
Beam after beam, upon the yielding night,
So teach and help me to sustain the sight.

NOON :—

"Take fast hold of instruction; let her not go."—*Prov.* iv. 13.

In all the little things of life,
 Thyself, Lord, may I see!
In little and in great alike,
 Reveal Thyself to me!

EVENING :—

What is my chief attraction to heaven?—(*Psa.* xvii. 15.)

Thy presence makes celestial day
 And fills each raptured soul with bliss;
Night would prevail, were God away,
 And spirits pine in Paradise.

JUNE 29.

MORNING:—

"I will triumph in the works of Thy hands."—*Psa.* xcii. 4.

> Thou who hast given me eyes to see,
>   And love this sight so fair,
> Give me a heart to find out Thee,
>   And read Thee everywhere.

NOON:—

"The earth is full of Thy riches."—*Psa.* civ. 24.

> Who would new-vest the green-robed earth,
>   Or crave of Heaven as boon
> A bluer sky, a brighter sun,
>   Or a serener moon?

EVENING:—

Do I know Christ as the God-man? (*John* i. 14, 16.)

> As man, He pities my complaint;
>   His power and truth are all divine;
> He will not fail, He cannot faint;
>   Lord, make Thy full salvation mine.

JUNE 30.

MORNING :—

"I will delight myself in Thy commandments, which I have loved."—*Psa*. cxix. 47.

So may Thy Spirit seal my soul,
    And mould it to Thy will,
That my fond heart no more may stray,
    But keep Thy covenant still.

NOON :—

"The knowledge of the Holy is understanding."—*Prov*. ix. 10.

Thee would I serve with soul and strength,
    On Thee through life depend;
Be Thou, O God, in life and death,
    My one eternal Friend.

EVENING :—

Do I rejoice in Christ as my Saviour?
—(*Luke* i. 47.)

A bleeding Saviour seen by faith,
    A sense of pardoning love,
A hope that triumphs over death,
    Give joys like those above.

JULY 1.

MORNING :—

"My heart shall rejoice in Thy salvation."—*Psa.* xiii. 5.

> I bless the Christ of God;
> I rest in love divine;
> And with unfaltering lip and heart,
> I call this Saviour mine.

NOON :—

"As the crackling of thorns under a pot, so is the laughter of the fool."—*Eccles.* vii. 6.

> Let not the joys Thy gospel gives
> A transient rapture prove,
> Nor let the world with smiles and frowns
> Our faith and hope remove.

EVENING :—

Is my joy in Christ a full and abiding joy?—(*John* xiv. 27.)

> Engage this roving treacherous heart;
> To fix on Mary's better part,
> To scorn the trifles of a day
> For joys that none can take away.

JULY 2.

MORNING :—

"What goodness the Lord shall do unto us, the same will we do unto thee."—*Numb.* x. 32.

    Thus may we abide in union
        With each other and the Lord,
    And possess, in sweet communion,
        Joys which earth can ne'er afford.

NOON :—

"The Lord hath spoken good concerning Israel."—*Numb.* x. 29.

    Come with us; we will do thee good,
        As God to us hath done;
    Stand but in Him, as those have stood
        Whose faith the victory won.

EVENING :—

Am I doing as I would be done by? —(*Matt.* vii. 12.)

    Have I in wealth forborne to spare
        A portion for the sons of need?
    Look'd coldly on the stranger's care?
        Or left the widow's heart to bleed?

JULY 3.

Morning:—

"We will go with you, for...God is with you."—*Zech.* viii. 23.

> Happy the Church, thou sacred place,
> The seat of thy Creator's grace;
> Thy holy courts are His abode,
> Thou earthly palace of our God.

Noon:—

"We know that we have passed from death unto life, because we love the brethren."—1 *John* iii. 14.

> I love Thy kingdom, Lord,
>   The house of Thine abode,
> The Church our blest Redeemer bought
>   With His most precious blood.

Evening:—

Have I cast in my lot with the people of God?—(*Heb.* xi. 25.)

> Oh may I see Thy tribes rejoice,
> And aid their triumphs with my voice!
> This is my glory, Lord, to be
> Join'd to Thy saints and near to Thee!

JULY 4

MORNING:—

"We will not forsake the house of our God."—*Neh*. x. 39.

> Being of beings! may our praise
>   Thy courts with grateful fragrance fill;
> Still may we stand before Thy face,
>   Still hear and do Thy sovereign will.

NOON:—

"A day in Thy courts is better than a thousand."—*Psa*. lxxxiv. 10.

> May we in faith receive Thy word,
>   In faith present our prayers,
> And in the presence of our Lord
>   Unbosom all our cares.

EVENING:—

Is there sin even in my worship?—(*Exod*. xxviii. 38.)

> Cold our services have been;
> Mingled, every prayer, with sin;
> But Thou canst and will forgive!
> By Thy grace alone we live.

JULY 8.

MORNING :—

"Herein do I exercise myself to have always a conscience void of offence."—*Acts* xxiv. 16.

 Order my footsteps by Thy word,
  And make my heart sincere;
 Let sin have no dominion, Lord,
  But keep my conscience clear.

NOON :—

"The thought of foolishness is sin."
—*Prov.* xxiv. 9.

 When not a fellow-man suspects
  That falsehood lurks within,
 Thine eye of purity detects
  Our hidden thought of sin.

EVENING :—

Are mine the fruits of the Spirit, or the works of the flesh ? (*Gal.* v. 19—23.)

 Has pride or wrath disturb'd my breast ?
  Or wishes wild and vain ?
 Has sinful sloth my powers possess'd,
  And bound them with its chain ?

JULY 6.

Morning :—

"I will not know a wicked person."
—*Psa.* ci. 4.

    Oh, may it be my constant choice
        To walk with men of grace below,
    Till I arrive where heavenly joys
        And never-fading honours grow.

Noon :—

"I said, Oh! that I had wings like a dove! for then would I fly away, and be at rest."—*Psa.* lv. 6.

    Ask not for the dove's swift pinion;
        Ask Heaven's Dove to come to thee;
    Ask for pardon's sweet oblivion;
        Ask for inward purity.

Evening :—

How can I endure to the end?—(*Gal.* v. 5.)

    Oh, who would bear life's stormy doom,
        Did not Thy wing of love
    Come brightly wafting through the gloom
        Our peace-branch from above?

JULY 7.

Morning :—

"I will take heed to my ways."—
Psa. xxxix. 1.

Let never man be bold enough to say,
Thus, and no further, shall my passions stray;
The first crime, past, compels us into more,
And guilt grows fast which was but choice
   before.

Noon :—

"The wise man's eyes are in his head, but the fool walketh in darkness."
—*Eccles.* ii. 14.

  One finger's breadth at hand will mar
   A world of light in heaven afar;
   A mote eclipse a glorious star;
    An eyelid hide the sky.

Evening :—

Am I a temple of the Holy Ghost?
—(1 *Cor.* iii. 16, 17.)

  Instruct me, rule me, guide my feet,
   My every thought control;
  My Teacher, Patron, Paraclete,
   Possess and guard my soul.

JULY 8.

MORNING:—

"The Lord is my Rock;...in Him will I trust."—2 *Sam.* xxii. 2, 3.

O God, whose thunder shakes the sky,
  Whose eye this atom-globe surveys,
To Thee, my only Rock, I fly,
  Thy mercy in Thy justice praise.

NOON:—

"The rich man's wealth is HIS strong city, and as an high wall in HIS OWN conceit."—*Prov.* xviii. 11.

O world, with all thy smiles and loves,
  With all thy song and wine,
What mockery of human hearts,
  What treachery is thine!

EVENING:—

Does my foot stand firm on the Rock of ages?—(*Psa.* xl. 2.)

  Here is firm footing; here,
    My soul, is solid rock,
  To break the waves of grief and fear,
    And trouble's rudest shock.

JULY 9.

MORNING :—

"Though He slay me, yet will I trust in Him."—*Job* xiii. 15.

 Why should I dread Jehovah's hand,
  Although it crush to dust?
 'Tis love that gives His arm command,
  And in that love I trust.

NOON :—

"Do good, O Lord, unto those that be good, and to them that are upright in their hearts."—*Psa.* cxxv. 4.

 In every state secure,
  Kept as Jehovah's eye,
 'Tis well with them while life endure,
  And well when call'd to die.

EVENING :—

Can I "trust" God where I cannot "trace" Him?—(*Job* xxxiii. 13.)

 What though thou tread with bleeding feet
  A thorny path of grief and gloom?
 Thy God will choose the way most meet
  To lead thee heavenward, lead thee home.

JULY 10.

MORNING:—

"Most gladly therefore will I rather glory in my infirmities."—2 *Cor.* xii. 9.

> On earth I covet not
>   That every wo should cease;
> Only, if trouble be my lot,
>   In Thee may I have peace.

NOON:—

"It is the Lord; let Him do what seemeth Him good."—1 *Sam.* iii. 18.

> Well may Thine own belov'd, who see
>   In all their lot their Father's pleasure,
> Bear loss of all they love, save Thee,
>   Their living, everlasting treasure.

EVENING:—

What comes as sorrow, can I "count" as joy?—(*James* i. 2.)

> Dear Father, we consent
>   To discipline divine,
> And bless the griefs which make our souls
>   Still more completely Thine.

JULY 11

MORNING:—

"I will greatly praise the Lord with my mouth."—*Psa*. cix. 30.

> My soul, triumphant in the Lord,
>   Shall tell its joys abroad,
> And march with holy vigour on,
>   Supported by its God.

NOON:—

"When thou goest, it shall lead thee; when thou sleepest, it shall keep thee."—*Prov*. vi. 22.

> Great God, let all my hours be Thine,
>   While I enjoy the light;
> Then shall my sun in smiles decline,
>   And bring a pleasant night.

EVENING:—

Am I one of God's Israel?—(*Gal*. vi. 16, *comp. Deut*. xxxiii. 29.)

> Glory to God, who Israel keeps,
> Who never slumbers, never sleeps;
> Almighty Power no weakness knows,
> Unwearied Love asks no repose.

JULY 12.

Morning :—

"I will praise Thee, O Lord my God, with all my heart."—*Psa.* lxxxvi. 12.

Oh, may Thy love inspire my tongue;
Salvation shall be all my song,
And all my powers shall join to bless
The Lord my Strength and Righteousness.

Noon :—

"Then shalt thou walk in thy way safely."—*Prov.* iii. 23.

Oh, let Thy grace inspire
  My soul with strength divine;
Let all my powers to Thee aspire,
  And all my days be Thine.

Evening :—

Whither do my desires rise?—(*Psa.* cxix. 113.)

Let me Thy power, Thy beauty, see;
  So shall my vain aspirings cease,
And my free heart shall follow Thee
  Through paths of everlasting peace.

JULY 13.

MORNING :—

"I will praise Thee for ever."—
Psa. lii. 9.

Lord, I will bless Thee all my days;
  Thy praise shall dwell upon my tongue;
My soul shall glory in Thy grace,
  While saints rejoice to hear the song.

NOON :—

"Here have we no continuing city, but we seek one to come."—*Heb.* xiii. 14.

Let come what may to me,
  It will, it must be blest;
Home in the distance I can see,
  And there shall be at rest.

EVENING :—

Whither do my footsteps tend?—
(*Heb.* xi. 15, 16.)

'Tis home, 'tis home, that we wish to reach;
  He who guides us may choose the way;
Little we heed what path we take,
  If nearer home each day.

JULY 14.

MORNING:—.

"Mine hand shall not be upon thee."
—1 *Sam.* xxiv. 12, 13.

Much forgiven, may I learn
Love for hatred to return;
Then assured my heart shall be,
Thou, my God, hast pardon'd me.

NOON:—

"Father, forgive them; for they know not what they do." *Luke* xxiii. 34.

Thy foes might hate, despise, revile;
Thy friends unfaithful prove;
Unwearied in forgiveness, still
Thy heart could only love.

EVENING:—

Do I love my enemies?—(*Matt.* v. 44.)

So does the fragrant sandal bow,
In meek forgiveness, to its doom,
And o'er the axe, at every blow,
Shed in abundance rich perfume.

JULY 15.

MORNING :—

"I will help thee;...let us behave ourselves valiantly."—1 *Chron.* xix. 12, 13.

> Help one another, help!
> The fainting heart revive;
> Lift up the fear-enfeebled hand;
> Keep dying hope alive.

NOON :—

"Safety (*marg.* victory) is of the Lord."—*Prov.* xxi. 31.

> Stand up, stand up for Jesus!
> The strife will not be long;
> This day, the noise of battle,—
> The next, the victor's song.

EVENING :—

Am I helpful to the weak, and do I sustain the falling?—(*Job* iv. 3, 4.)

> O happy, happy, who love's task fulfil,
> Who their true loving Lord do copy still,
> And for Love's sake by Love do execute
> Love's will.

JULY 16.

MORNING:—

"I will surely show thee kindness for...thy father's sake."—2 *Sam.* ix. 7.

> Thy father's friend forsake not,
> But show him kindness due;
> And summer-friends mistake not
> For the ever-faithful few.

NOON:—

"The memory of the just is blessed."
—*Prov.* x. 7.

Lov'd while on earth! nor less belov'd tho'
  Think not I envy you your crown. [gone!
  No! if I could, I would not call you down;
Tho' slower is my pace, to you I follow on.

EVENING:—

Am I following those who have gone before to glory?—(*Heb.* vi. 11, 12.)

> I'll follow on,
> Leaning on Jesus all the way,
> Who now and then lets fall a ray
> Of comfort from His throne.

JULY 17.

Morning:—

"Daniel purposed...that he would not defile himself."—*Dan.* i. 8.

> O for a persevering power
> To keep Thy just commands!
> We would defile our hearts no more,
> No more pollute our hands.

Noon:—

"In malice, be ye children; but in understanding, be men." 1 *Cor.*xiv.20.

> Keep, Lord, our souls for ever young,
> For ever undefiled;
> Nor let the gifts of manhood drown
> The graces of the child.

Evening:—

Does my soul need cleansing?—(1 *John* i. 7.)

> Jesus, my great High-priest, has died;
> I seek no sacrifice beside;
> His blood did once for all atone,
> And now He pleads before the throne.

JULY 18.

Morning:—

"As for me, I will walk in mine integrity."—*Psa.* xxvi. 11.

Lord, I my vows to Thee renew;
Disperse my sins as morning dew;
Guard my first springs of thought and will,
And with Thyself my spirit fill.

Noon:—

"A sound heart is the life of the flesh."—*Prov.* xiv. 30.

My cares, I give you to the wind,
 And shake you off like dust;
Well may I trust my all with Him
 With whom my soul I trust.

Evening:—

Does my soul need refreshing?—(*Deut.* xxxii. 2.)

Oh, speak a blessing, gracious Lord;
 Thy blessing has a soothing power;
On toil-worn hearts Thy gentle word
 Falls softly as the evening shower.

JULY 19.

MORNING :—

"I hate the work of them that turn aside; it shall not cleave to me."—*Psa.* ci. 3.

> Oh, may I ne'er to evil yield,
>   Defended from above,
> And kept and covered by the shield
>   Of Thine almighty love.

NOON :—

"Slothfulness casteth into a deep sleep."—*Prov.* xix. 15.

> Oh, sleep not thou as others do;
>   Awake, be vigilant, be brave!
> The coward, and the sluggard too,
>   Must wear the fetters of the slave.

EVENING :—

Does my soul need rousing? (1 *Thess.* v. 6—10.)

> Come, Holy Spirit, heavenly Dove,
>   With all Thy quickening powers;
> Come, shed abroad a Saviour's love,
>   And that shall kindle ours.

JULY 20.

Morning:—

"O Lord, to Thee will I cry."— *Joel* i. 19.

> Not a throb but Thou canst feel,
> Not a pain but Thou canst heal,
> Not a pulse of mortal grief,
> But Thou know'st to bring relief.

Noon:—

"Where the word of a king is, there is power."—*Eccles.* viii. 4.

> When Mercy spoke in low small voice,
>   "Ye waters, peace, be still!"
> The billows sank, the winds were hush'd,
>   Obedient to THAT will!

Evening:—

Do trials make me distrustful of Christ's love?—(*Mark* iv. 38.)

> Wakes the storm? it is to try thee,
>   Sleeps the Christ? 'tis for thy sake.
> Let the heart but feel Him nigh thee,
>   Lift thy voice, and He'll awake.

JULY 21.

MORNING :—

"As for me, I will come into Thy house in the multitude of Thy mercy."
—*Psa.* v. 7.

> 'Mid worldly commotion,
> My wearied heart faints
> For the house of devotion,
> The home of Thy saints.

NOON :—

"The Lord is my Shepherd, I shall not want."—*Psa.* xxiii. 1.

> Shepherd of souls, refresh and bless
> Thy chosen pilgrim-flock,
> With manna in the wilderness,
> With water from the rock.

EVENING :—

Do I guard against "guilty gloom"?
—(*John* xiv. 1.)

> Holy Ghost, dispel our sadness,
> Pierce the clouds of sinful night;
> Come, Thou Source of sweetest gladness,
> Breathe Thy life, and spread Thy light.

JULY 22.

MORNING:—

"O God, Thou art my God; early will I seek Thee."—*Psa.* lxiii. 1.

> Never from the gates of prayer
> Turn with doubting sorrow;
> For the One who standeth there,
> May answer you to-morrow.

NOON:—

"For Thy name's sake, lead me and guide me."—*Psa.* xxxi. 3.

> "Lord, for Thy name's sake!"—Such the plea,
> With force triumphant fraught,
> By which Thy saints prevail with Thee,
> By thine own Spirit taught.

EVENING:—

If comfortless, has it not been my own fault?—(2 *Cor.* i. 3, 4.)

> Cheer'd with Thy converse, I can trace
> The desert with delight;
> Through all the gloom one smile of Thine
> Can dissipate the night.

JULY 23.

MORNING:—

"Let us search and try our ways, and turn again to the Lord."—*Lam.* iii. 40.

> Thus melt us down, thus make us bend,
> And Thy dominion own,
> Nor let a rival more pretend
> To re-possess Thy throne.

NOON:—

"Turn you at My reproof."—*Prov.* i. 23.

> Lord, I come to Thee for rest;
> Take possession of my breast;
> There Thy blood-bought right maintain,
> And without a rival reign.

EVENING:—

Have I laid down the weapons of rebellion against God?—(1 *Pet.* v. 6.)

> Now let me search and try my ways,
> And prostrate seek His face;
> Conscious of guilt, before His throne
> In dust my soul abase.

JULY 24.

MORNING:—

"By Thee only will we make mention of Thy name."—*Isa.* xxvi. 13.

> Give us hearts to scorn all pleasure
>   That would tempt our steps aside;
> Be Thy smile our single treasure,
>   And Thy blessed voice our guide.

NOON:—

"Come, eat of My bread, and drink of the wine which I have mingled."—*Prov.* ix. 5.

> O voice of mercy, voice of love!
>   In conflict, grief, and agony,
> Support me, cheer me from above,
>   And gently whisper, "Come to Me."

EVENING:—

Do I know Christ as my Shepherd? —(*John* x. 14.)

> I was a wandering sheep,
>   I would not be controll'd;
> But now I love my Shepherd's voice,
>   I love, I love the fold.

JULY 25.

MORNING:—

"So will not we go back from Thee."—*Psa.* lxxx. 18.

The world without may rage, but we
Will only cling more close to Thee,
With hearts to Thee more wholly given,
More wean'd from earth, more fix'd on heaven.

NOON:—

"Trust in the Lord with all thine heart."—*Prov.* iii. 5.

When our foes and fears alarm us,
  And the heart with grief o'erflows,
Then how sweet the voice that bids us
  On the Saviour's love repose!

EVENING:—

Do I use the world without abusing it?—(*James* iv. 4.)

Gold, learning, glory—what are they
  Without the faith that looks on high
The sand-forts of a child at play,
  Which "are not" when the wave goes by.

JULY 26.

Morning:—

"I have sworn...that I will keep Thy righteous judgments."—*Psa.* cxix. 106.

> Oh, may I live on Jesus still,
>   And use the talents given,
> Daily consult and do His will,
>   And thus prepare for heaven.

Noon:—

"I have sworn, and I will perform it."—*Ibid.*

> Lord, Thou hast made me know Thy ways!
>   Conduct me in Thy fear!
> And grant me such supplies of grace
>   That I may persevere.

Evening:—

Do I joy in a promise-keeping God? —(*Heb.* x. 23.)

> Thy promise shall be to my soul
>   A messenger sent from the skies,
> An anchor when billows shall roll,
>   A refuge when tempests arise.

JULY 27.

MORNING :—

"I will walk within my house with a perfect heart."—*Psa.* ci. 2.

> Pure may I be, averse to sin,
> Just, holy, merciful, and true;
> And let Thine image, form'd within,
> Shine out in all I speak and do.

NOON :—

"A faithful man shall abound with blessings."—*Prov.* xxviii. 20.

> Happy the home when God is there,
> And love fills every breast;
> When one their wish, and one their prayer,
> And one their heavenly rest.

EVENING :—

Am I thankful to God for my home-mercies?—(*Psa.* cxviii. 15.)

> And, oh! if homes like these be sweet,
> How sweet that home must be,
> Where all the ransom'd ones shall meet,
> From sin and sorrow free.

JULY 28.

MORNING :—

"My righteousness I hold fast, and will not let it go."—*Job* xxvii. 6.

> Hold on thy course, O weary soul,
> Hold on thine upward way;
> Leave not the rugged road of right,
> In smoother paths to stray.

NOON :—

"One generation passeth away, and another generation cometh."—*Eccles.* i. 4.

> Soon will this toilsome strife be o'er,
> Of sorrow and of care,
> And life's dull vanities no more
> This anxious breast ensnare.

EVENING :—

Do I improve the calm of eventide?—(*Gen.* xxiv. 63.)

Oft as this peaceful hour shall come,
Lord, raise my thoughts from earthly things,
And bear them to my heavenly home
On faith and hope's celestial wings.

JULY 29.

MORNING:—

"I will sing, yea, I will sing praises unto the Lord."—*Psa.* xxvii. 6.

Help, ye bright angelic spirits,
  Bring your sweetest, noblest lays,
Help to sing our Saviour's merits,
  Help to chant Immanuel's praise.

NOON:—

"Thou wast slain, and hast redeemed us to God by Thy blood."—*Rev.* v. 9.

And shall not he the chorus join
  Whose form the Incarnate Godhead wore,
Whose guilt, whose fears, whose triumph tell
  How deep the wounds the Saviour bore?

EVENING:—

Have I access to a fulness of blessing?—(*Col.* i. 19.)

His grace through all the desert flows,
  An unexhausted stream;
That grace on Zion's sacred mount
  Shall be my endless theme.

JULY 30.

MORNING:—

"I will sing praise to my God, while I have my being."—*Psa*.civ.33.

> Begin, ye saints, the joyful task;
> Let praise employ your tongue,
> Until eternity shall ask
> A more exalted song.

NOON:—

"I am my Beloved's, and my Beloved is mine."—*S. Song* vi. 3.

> Let the sweet hope that Thou art mine,
> My life and death attend,—
> Thy presence through my journey shine,
> And crown the journey's end.

EVENING:—

Have I a life-long cause for joy?— (*Psa*. v. 11.)

> O Lord, I would delight in Thee,
> And on Thy care depend,
> To Thee in every trouble flee,
> My best, my only Friend.

JULY 31.

Morning:—
"I will sing with the spirit, and I will sing with the understanding also."—1 *Cor.* xiv. 15.

> Oh, let a sense of grace divine
>   My best affections move,
> That while my lips Thy praise proclaim,
>   My heart may feel Thy love.

Noon:—
"Let my Beloved come into His garden, and eat His pleasant fruits."—*S. Song* iv. 16.

> Like trees of myrrh and spice we stand,
> Planted by God the Father's hand;
> And all His springs in Zion flow
> To make the young plantation grow.

Evening:—
Are my songs of praise more than lip-service?—(*Eph.* v. 19.)

> Sing we, till we feel our hearts
>   Ascending with our tongues;
> Sing, till the love of sin departs,
>   And grace inspires our songs.

AUGUST 1.

Morning:—

"I am resolved what to do."—*Luke* xvi. 4.

> A charge to keep I have;
> A God to glorify;
> A never-dying soul to save,
> And fit it for the sky.

Noon:—

"The children of this world are in their generation wiser than the children of light."—*Luke* xvi. 8.

> While carnal men with all their might
> Earth's vanities pursue,
> How slow the advances which I make
> With heaven itself in view!

Evening:—

Do I carry out the resolutions I make?—(*Deut.* xxiii. 21, 23.)

> My soul, what hast thou done for God?
> Look o'er thy mis-spent years, and see;
> Sum up what thou hast done for Him,
> And then what God hath done for thee.

AUGUST 2.

MORNING:—

"This I do for the gospel's sake."—
1 *Cor*. ix. 23 (*comp*. 22).

When weaker Christians we despise,
　We do the gospel mighty wrong;
For God, the gracious and the wise,
　Receives the feeble with the strong.

NOON:—

"Learn of Me; for I am meek and lowly in heart."—*Matt*. xi. 29.

Jesus, to us the grace impart
　Which shone so bright in Thee;
The humble, meek, and lowly heart,
　From pride and envy free.

EVENING:—

Do I ever waive my own rights?—
(1 *Cor*. ix. 12.)

Daily, bless'd Spirit, lay my heart
　All open to my view;
And, with Thy healing, quickening grace,
　That heart each day renew.

AUGUST 3.

MORNING :—

"Thou hast fully KNOWN my doctrine, manner of life, PURPOSE, faith, longsuffering, charity, patience."—*Tim.* iii. 10.

> So let our lips and lives express
> The holy gospel we profess;
> So let our works and virtues shine
> To prove the doctrine all divine.

NOON :—

"The just man walketh in his integrity."—*Prov.* xx. 7.

> Thou holy God, preserve my soul
>   From all pollution free!
> The pure in heart are Thy delight,
>   And they Thy face shall see.

EVENING :—

Am I an epistle of Christ read and known?—(2 *Cor.* iii. 2, 3.)

> Has grace, descending from above,
>   This evil heart possess'd,
> In meekness, patience, truth, and love,
>   To all around express'd?

AUGUST 4.

MORNING:—

"I will look unto the Lord; I will wait for the God of my salvation."—*Mic.* vii. 7.

> Christian, cast an eye above thee,
> Thou hast yet a Friend to love thee;
> Jesus shall forsake thee never;
> He will be thy strength for ever.

NOON:—

"His secret is with the righteous."—*Prov.* iii. 32.

> The Lord shall make him know
> The secrets of His heart,
> The wonders of His covenant show,
> And all His love impart.

EVENING:—

Do I know Christ as the Way of salvation?—(*John* xiv. 6.)

> Thou art the Way;—to Thee alone
> From sin and death we flee;
> And he who would the Father seek,
> Must seek Him, Lord, in Thee.

AUGUST 5.

MORNING:—

"Though an host should encamp against me, my heart shall not fear."—*Psa.* xxvii. 3.

> Now let the feeble all be strong,
> And make Jehovah's arm their song;
> His shield is spread o'er every saint,
> And, thus supported, who shall faint?

NOON:—

"In all thy ways acknowledge Him, and He shall direct thy paths."—*Prov.* iii. 6.

> Lord! through the Spirit whom Thy Son
>   Hath bidden us in prayer to ask,
> Arm us with might, that every task
> Whate'er we do, in Thee be done.

EVENING:—

Do I know Christ as the truth from heaven?—(*John* viii. 31, 32.)

> Thou art the Truth;—Thy word alone
>   True wisdom can impart;
> Thou only canst instruct the mind,
>   And purify the heart.

AUGUST 6.

MORNING:—

"Though I walk through the valley of the shadow of death, I will fear no evil."—*Psa.* xxiii. 4.

> Blessed who in Christ shall die,
>   Death is changed to life for ever!
> They have life when death is nigh;
>   Life beyond, which endeth never!

NOON:—

"The living know that they shall die."—*Eccles.* ix. 5.

> Lord! it is not life—to live,
>   If Thy presence Thou deny.
> Lord, if Thou Thy presence give,
>   'Tis no longer death—to die.

EVENING:—

Do I know Christ as the Life?—(1 *John* v. 12.)

> Thou art the Life;—the rending tomb
>   Proclaims Thy conquering arm;
> And those who put their trust in Thee,
>   Nor death nor hell shall harm.

AUGUST 7.

MORNING:—

"I will follow Thee whithersoever Thou goest."—*Matt.* viii. 19.

> Omnipotence is on your side,
>   And wisdom watches o'er your head,
> Yea, God Himself will be your guide,
>   So ye but follow where He leads.

NOON:—

"Thy foot shall not stumble."—*Prov.* iii. 23.

> Guard me, Saviour, by Thy power;
> Guard me in the trying hour;
> Let Thine unremitted care
> Save me from the lurking snare.

EVENING:—

Do I fix my eye on Him I follow? —(*Eph.* v. 1, 2.)

> Oh, keep the morning of His incarnation,
> The burning noon-tide of His bitter passion,
> The night of His descending, and the height
> Of His ascension, ever in my sight!

AUGUST 8.

MORNING:—

"Though I should die with Thee, yet will I not deny Thee."—*Matt.* xxvi. 35.

> Deny Thee! what, deny the way
> That leads to heaven's eternal day?
> Deny Thee, who alone canst give
> The hope that bids the sinner live?

NOON:—

"The servant is not greater than his lord."—*John* xv. 20.

> Why should I court my Master's foe;
>   Why should I fear its frown?
> Why should I seek for rest below,
>   Or sigh for brief renown?

EVENING:—

What if I am led by a dark and thorny road?—(*Heb.* ii. 10.)

> Lord, should my path through suffering lie,
>   Forbid it I should e'er repine;
> Still let me turn to Calvary,
>   Nor heed my griefs, remembering Thine.

AUGUST 9.

Morning :—

"I will lay down my life for Thy sake."—*John* xiii. 37.

> Alas! a deeper test of faith,
>   Than prison-cell or martyr's stake,
> The self-abasing watchfulness
>   Of silent prayer may make.

Noon :—

"Couldst not thou watch one hour?"—*Mark* xiv. 37.

> Bright hopes that erst the bosom warm'd,
> And vows too pure to be perform'd,
> And prayers blown wide by gales of care,
> Wandering and broken all, athwart the conscience glare.

Evening :—

Should repeated failures lead me to despair?—(*Prov.* xxiv. 16.)

> Many are our falls, and grievous;
>   Oh, let this truth abase our heart;
> But Thou wilt ne'er forsake or leave us;
>   Let this, Thy mercy, strength impart.

AUGUST 10.

MORNING:—

"With my song will I praise Him."
—*Psa.* xxviii. 7.

> Father, how wide Thy glory shines!
> How high Thy wonders rise!
> Known through the earth by thousand signs,
> By thousands through the skies!

NOON:—

"He is thy praise, and He is thy God."—*Deut.* x. 21.

> The Son of God, the Lord of life,
> How wondrous are His ways!
> O for a harp of thousand strings
> To sound abroad His praise.

EVENING:—

Do I honour the Holy Spirit?—(*Eph.* iv. 30.)

> Praises to Him who sheds abroad
> Within our hearts the love of God,
> The Spirit of all truth and peace,
> Fountain of joy and holiness.

AUGUST 11.

Morning:—

"His praise shall continually be in my mouth."—*Psa.* xxxiv. 1.

How would I praise Thee, Lord, how would my rhymes
   Gladly engrave Thy love in steel,
If what my soul doth feel sometimes,
   My soul might ever feel.

Noon:—

"The valleys...are covered over with corn."—*Psa.* lxv. 13.

His covenant with the earth He keeps;
   My tongue, His goodness sing!
Summer and Winter know their time;
   And Harvest crowns the Spring.

Evening:—

Am I ripening for heaven?—(*Matt.* xiii. 30, 39.)

Another harvest comes apace!
Ripen our spirits by Thy grace,
That we may calmly meet the blow
The sickle gives to lay us low.

AUGUST 12.

MORNING:—

"I will greatly rejoice in the Lord; my soul shall be joyful in my God."—*Isa.* lxi. 10.

Oh, let the dead now hear Thy voice:
Now bid Thy banish'd ones rejoice;
Their beauty this, their glorious dress,
Jesus, the Lord our Righteousness.

NOON:—

"He hath covered me with the robe of righteousness."—*Ibid.*

Sing how He left the heavenly throne,
  And laid His splendid robes aside,
Put all our mortal weakness on,
  And toil'd and suffer'd, wept and died.

EVENING:—

Do I keep the white robe unspotted?
—(*Rev.* iii. 4.)

With care I guard that raiment white
  In which to meet my Father's face;
And, soon as sinful stain appears,
  I hasten to the Fount of grace.

AUGUST 13.

MORNING:—

"I also will requite you this kindness, because ye have done this thing."
—2 *Sam*. ii. 6.

> While grateful to the Lord above,
>   Whose gracious hand you own,
> Requite the services of love,
>   By fellow-mortals shown.

NOON:—

"The recompence of a man's hands shall be rendered unto him." *Prov*.xii.14.

> As done for Thee, do Thou receive
>   Each humble work of mine;
> Worth to my meanest labour give
>   By joining it to Thine.

EVENING:—

If the reward tarry, do I wait for it?
—(*Heb*. x. 37.)

> It is not yet perchance, nor here
>   Their hope and blessing shall be given,
> Through loneliness, and pain, and fear,
>   Who faithfully have striven.

AUGUST 14.

MORNING:—

"I will not be burdensome to you; for I seek not yours, but you."—2 *Cor.* xii. 14.

> Jesus, I fain would find
> Thy zeal for God in me,
> Thy yearning pity for mankind,
> Thy burning charity.

NOON:—

"The love of money is the root of all evil."—1 *Tim.* vi. 10.

> Oh, wean my heart from too much care
> Of what belongs to earthly things,
> From hopes that end but in despair,
> From false and vain imaginings.

EVENING:—

Is earthly wealth dearer to me than heavenly?—(*Matt.* vi. 19—21.)

> Raise thy repining eyes, and take true mea-
> Of thine eternal treasure;   [sure
> The Father of thy Lord can grudge thee
> The world for thee was bought.   [nought;

AUGUST 15.

MORNING:—

"If meat make my brother to offend, I will eat no flesh while the world standeth."—1 *Cor.* viii. 13.

> May we to others stoop, and learn
>   To emulate Thy love;
> So shall we bear Thine image here,
>   And share Thy throne above.

NOON:—

"All things are not expedient."— 1 *Cor.* x. 23.

> Oh, let me think how Thou didst leave
>   Untasted every pure delight,
> To fast, to faint, to watch, to grieve,
>   The toilsome day, the homeless night.

EVENING:—

Is self dearer to me than the good of souls?—(*Phil.* ii. 20, 21.)

> Let grace our selfishness expel,
>   Our earthliness refine,
> And kindness in our bosoms dwell
>   As free and true as Thine.

AUGUST 16.

MORNING:—

"It is good for me to draw near to God."—*Psa.* lxxiii. 28.

> When thus in simple faith we dare
> Our empty urn to bring,
> Oh, nerve the feeble hand of prayer
> To dip it in the spring.

NOON:—

"God is the strength of my heart."—*Psa.* lxxiii. 26.

> Am I drooping? Thou art near me,
> Near to bear me on my way.
> Am I pleading? Thou wilt hear me,
> Hear and answer, when I pray.

EVENING:—

Do I grudge the time spent in prayer?—(*Luke* ii. 37.)

> I love, when I am weary,
> And faint and worn, and sad,
> To spend an hour with Jesus,
> Whose presence makes me glad.

AUGUST 17.

MORNING:—

"I will pay my vows...in the courts of the Lord's house." *Psa.* cxvi. 18, 19.

> Pleasant are Thy courts above,
> In the land of light and love;
> Pleasant are Thy courts below,
> In this land of sin and wo.

NOON:—

"We have boldness and access with confidence by the faith of Him."— *Eph.* iii. 12.

> My soul, oppress'd with guilt and fear,
> Can through this living way draw near;
> The full atonement made for sin
> Spreads peace and solid joy within.

EVENING:—

Do I doubt God's willingness to hear my cry?—(*Isa.* xxx. 19.)

> Refuse to hear the heartfelt prayer,
> Or feel for all His people's care?
> The stars as soon will cease to glow,
> Or ocean's tides refuse to flow.

AUGUST 18.

MORNING :—

"I will now say, Peace be within thee."—*Psa*. cxxii. 8.

> Then shall each age and rank agree
>   United shouts of joy to raise;
> And Zion, made a praise by Thee,
>   To Thee shall render back the praise.

NOON :—

"We which have believed do enter into rest."—*Heb*. iv. 3.

> Thine earthly Sabbaths, Lord, we love,
> But there's a nobler rest above;
> To that our labouring souls aspire
> With ardent hope and strong desire.

EVENING :—

Do I cultivate a Sabbath-spirit through the week ?—(*Psa*. xxvii. 4.)

> Father, my soul would still abide
> Within Thy temple, near Thy side;
> But if my feet must hence depart,
> Still keep Thy dwelling in my heart.

AUGUST 19.

Morning:—

"Let my soul live, and it shall praise Thee."—*Psa.* cxix. 175.

> Praise to Thee, Thou great Creator;
>   Praise be Thine from every tongue;
> Join my soul with every creature,
>   Join the universal song.

Noon:—

"He that feareth the commandment shall be in peace."—*Prov.* xiii. 13, (*marg.*).

> The heart that trusts for ever sings,
> And feels as light as it had wings;
> A well of peace within it springs,
>   Come good or ill.

Evening:—

Is mine a true or a false peace?— (*Isa.* lvii. 19—21.)

> When the soft dews of kindly sleep
> My wearied eyelids gently steep,
> Be my last thought how sweet to rest
> For ever on my Saviour's breast!

AUGUST 20.

MORNING:—

"I will praise Thee, for Thou hast heard me."—*Psa*. cxviii. 21.

> Thou givest more than human hearts
> Have faith to wish their own;
> More than we ask or e'en desire
> Comes from Thy love alone.

NOON:—

"The desire accomplished is sweet to the soul."—*Prov*. xiii. 19.

> To take a glimpse within the veil,
> To know that God is mine.
> Are springs of joy that never fail,
> Unspeakable, divine.

EVENING:—

Is my heart renewed or unrenewed? —(*Eph*. iv. 23, &c.)

> Oh for a heart to praise my God,
> A heart from sin set free,
> A heart that's sprinkled with the blood
> So freely shed for me.

AUGUST 21.

MORNING :—

"I will extol Thee, O Lord; for Thou hast lifted me up."—*Psa.* xxx. 1.

I bent before Thy gracious throne,
  And asked for peace, on suppliant knee;
And peace was given, nor peace alone,
  But faith sublimed to ecstasy.

NOON :—

"He that keepeth understanding, shall find good."—*Prov.* xix. 8.

Awake our souls, and bless His name
  Whose mercies never fail,
Who opens wide a door of hope
  In Achor's gloomy vale.

EVENING :—

Is my will subdued or rebellious?—(*Heb.* xii. 9.)

Through all my trials here,
  Be Thou my stay, O Holy One,
And—be my portion weal or wo—
  Help me to say, "Thy will be done."

AUGUST 22.

MORNING :—

"Thy people shall be my people, and thy God my God."—*Ruth* i. 16.

> They say thy God in heaven above
>   Can comfort when the heart is sore;
> Then Him thou lovest let me love
>   For evermore.

NOON :—

"The fashion of this world passeth away."—1 *Cor.* vii. 31.

> Before the sun declineth
>   Thy course may ended be;
> And when again it shineth,
>   It may not shine on thee.

EVENING :—

Are earthly affections ensnaring my soul?—(1 *John* ii. 17.)

> Where the smile shall ever stay,
> No loved glance pass away,
> Nor the cherished face grow pale,
> Nor the tones of fondness fail,
>   There be my home!

AUGUST 23.

MORNING:—

"I have chosen the way of truth."
—*Psa*. cxix. 30.

    O let the love of sacred truth
      Our erring souls, O God, inspire,
    And the blest paths of holiness
      Be all our aim and our desire.

NOON:—

"A good name is rather to be chosen than great riches."—*Prov*. xxii. 1.

    I choose the path of heavenly truth,
      And glory in my choice;
    Not all the riches of the earth
      Could make me so rejoice.

EVENING:—

Do I value my character above my purse?—(*Eccles*. vii. 1.)

    Judge me, O Lord, and try my heart,
      For Thou that heart canst see;
    And bid each idol thence depart
      That dares compete with Thee.

AUGUST 24.

MORNING:—

"I keep under my body, and bring it into subjection."—1 *Cor.* ix. 27.

 I'd part with all the joys of sense
  To gaze upon Thy throne ;
 Pleasure springs fresh for ever thence,
  Unspeakable, unknown.

NOON :—

"So run that ye may obtain."—1 *Cor.* ix. 24.

 Bless'd Saviour, introduced by Thee,
  Have I my race begun ;
 And, crown'd with victory, at Thy feet
  I'll lay my honours down.

EVENING :—

Do I overvalue the esteem of men? —(*John* v. 44.)

 He bore God's curse thy soul to save,—
 And fearest thou man's wrath to brave?
 He bore the cross,—wilt thou refuse
 To bear the cross His love shall choose?

AUGUST 25.

MORNING:—

"My soul is cast down within me; therefore will I remember Thee."—*Psa.* xlii. 6.

> Take courage, O my soul, nor steep
>   Thy days and nights in tears;
> Soon shalt thou cease to mourn and weep,
>   Though dark are now thy fears.

NOON:—

"Unto the upright there ariseth light in the darkness."—*Psa.* cxii. 4.

> Oft I walk beneath the cloud,
> Dark as midnight's gloomy shroud;
> But when fear is at its height,
> Jesus comes, and all is light.

EVENING:—

Do I let patience have her perfect work?—(*James* i. 4.)

> In silence will I bear the pain
>   Which God has sent me by His will;
> Ne'er will I murmur or complain;
>   Although He wound, He loves me still.

AUGUST 26.

MORNING:—

"Surely I will remember Thy wonders of old."—*Psa.* lxxvii. 11.

> Praise Him for His grace and favour
>   To our fathers in distress;
> Praise Him, still the same for ever,
>   Slow to chide and swift to bless.

NOON:—

"I have loved thee with an everlasting love."—*Jer.* xxxi. 3.

> Gather at length my weary soul
>   To join Thy saints above;
> For I would learn a song of praise
>   Eternal as Thy love.

EVENING:—

Do I let affliction work its appointed end?—(*John* xv. 2.)

> A bruised reed He will not break;
>   Afflictions all His children feel;
> He wounds them for His mercy's sake;
>   He wounds to heal.

AUGUST 27.

MORNING:—

"I will make Thy name to be remembered."—*Psa.* xlv. 17.

> We know Emmanuel's name,
>   Our hearts have loved it long,
> And dying sires bequeath'd His fame,
>   To be their children's song.

NOON:—

"His banner over me was love."—*S. Song* ii. 4.

> O love of God, our shield and stay
> Through all the perils of our way,
> Eternal love, in thee we rest,
> For ever safe, for ever blest.

EVENING:—

Do I listen to Christ's fear-silencing words?—(*John* vi. 20.)

> Oh, speak once more that word of peace,
>   And smooth this ruffled breast,
> Bid all its dark forebodings cease,
>   And hush its griefs to rest.

AUGUST 28.

MORNING:—

"My mouth shall speak the praise of the Lord."—*Psa.* cxlv. 21.

Wide as the world is His command,
   Vast as eternity His love,
Firm as a rock His truth shall stand
   When rolling years shall cease to move.

NOON:—

"Awake up, my glory; awake, psaltery and harp."—*Psa.* lvii. 8.

While harps unnumber'd sound His praise
   In yonder world above,
His saints on earth admire His ways,
   And glory in His love.

EVENING:—

Am I one with the saints in glory?—(*Heb.* xii. 22, 23.)

Ah, Lord, with tardy steps I creep,
And sometimes sing, and sometimes weep;
Yet strip me of this house of clay,
And I will sing as loud as they.

AUGUST 29.

MORNING :—

"With my mouth will I make known Thy faithfulness to all generations."—*Psa.* lxxxix. 1.

> Though mountains crumble into dust,
>   Thy covenant standeth fast;
> Who follows Thee in pious trust
>   Shall reach Thy home at last.

NOON :—

"He will ever be mindful of His covenant."—*Psa.* cxi. 5.

> The tide of time shall never
>   His covenant remove;
> His name shall stand for ever;
>   That name to us is Love.

EVENING :—

Do I take God at His word?—(*John* iii. 33.)

> Yes, since God Himself has said it,
>   On the promise I rely;
> His good word demands my credit;
>   What can unbelief reply?

AUGUST 30.

MORNING:—

"My mouth shall show forth Thy righteousness and Thy salvation all the day."—*Psa.* lxxi. 15.

> Praise with my heart, my mind, my voice,
>   For all Thy mercy I will give;
> My heart shall still in God rejoice,
>   My tongue shall bless Thee while I live.

NOON:—

"He satisfieth the longing soul."—*Psa.* cvii. 9.

> O world, produce a good like this,
>   And thou shalt have my love;
> Till then my Father claims it all,
>   And Christ who dwells above.

EVENING:—

Is my Bible read or unread?—(*Acts* xvii. 11.)

> Great God, mine eyes with pleasure look
> On the dear volume of Thy book;
> There my Redeemer's face I see,
> And read His name who died for me.

AUGUST 31.

MORNING :—

"I will remember the years of the right hand of the Most High."—*Psa.* lxxvii. 10.

   Grief may come, but shall not whelm thee,
     Joy may come, but shall not harm,
   If they both shall find thee leaning
     On the everlasting arm.

NOON :—

"The righteous shall flourish as a branch."—*Prov.* xi. 28.

   "Abide in Me;"—then shall your leaves
     Be fresh, and green, and fair,
   And every richly-laden bough
     A goodly fruitage bear.

EVENING :—

Are my motives pure?—(*Phil.* i. 15—17.)

   Control my every thought,
     My every sin remove,
   Let all my works in Thee be wrought,
     Let all be wrought in love.

SEPTEMBER 1.

MORNING:—
" Return unto thy rest, O my soul."
—*Psa*. cxvi. 7.

In the ark the weary dove
　Found a welcome resting-place;
Thus my spirit longs to prove
　Rest in Christ, the ark of grace.

NOON:—
" The backslider in heart shall be filled with his own ways."—*Prov*. xiv. 14.

Why should my foolish passions rove?
　Where can such sweetness be,
As I have tasted in Thy love,
　As I have found in Thee?

EVENING:—
Am I bringing forth fruit to myself?
—(*Hos*. x. 1.)

Let Thy love my heart inflame,
　Keep Thy fear before my sight,
Be Thy praise my highest aim,
　Be Thy smile my chief delight.

SEPTEMBER 2.

MORNING:—

"I will pay my vows before them that fear Him."—*Psa.* xxii. 25.

> What shall I render to my God
>   For all His kindness shown?
> My feet shall visit Thine abode,
>   My songs address Thy throne.

NOON:—

"Thy vows are upon me, O God."—*Psa.* lvi. 12.

> My God, my King, Thy praise I sing,
>   My heart is all Thine own;
> My highest powers, my choicest hours,
>   I yield to Thee alone.

EVENING:—

Am I cherishing no known sin?—(*Psa.* xix. 12, 13.)

> Is there a thing beneath the sun
>   That strives with Thee my heart to share?
> Ah, tear it thence, and reign alone
>   The Lord of every motion there.

SEPTEMBER 3.

MORNING:—

"Thy servant will go and fight."—
1 *Sam.* xvii. 32.

> Go forth undaunted;—ever bear
>   A fearless heart where danger springs;
> For, oh, remember thou dost wear
>   The armour of the King of kings.

NOON:—

"The Lord God is a sun and shield."—*Psa.* lxxxiv. 11.

> God is thy shield, thy sun-like shield,
>   And He, thy sword of power;
> He saves thee in the battle-field
>   Through danger's darkest hour.

EVENING:—

If alone in the Christian life, is not Jesus with me?—(1 *John* iv. 4.)

> Fighting alone to-night!
>   With what a sinking heart!
> Lord Jesus, in the fight
>   Oh, stand not Thou apart!

SEPTEMBER 4.

MORNING:—

"I will go in the strength of the Lord God."—*Psa.* lxxi. 16.

> Yes, Lord, I must; yes, Lord, I will;
>   If Thou wilt lead me home,
> Strong in Thy strength, I'll fear no ill,
>   But fight and overcome.

NOON:—

"When I am weak, then am I strong."—2 *Cor.* xii. 10.

> Unto Thee for help I seek;
>   Perfect, Lord, Thy strength in me;
> I am strong when I am weak;
>   Weak myself, but strong in Thee.

EVENING:—

If alone in the world, have I not a Father in heaven?—(*John* viii. 29.)

> I am weak, yet strong;
> I murmur not that Thou bereavest me;
> Lone, weak, and helpless, I the more belong,
>   Father Supreme, to Thee.

SEPTEMBER 5.

MORNING :—

"I will not trust in my bow, neither shall my sword save me." *Psa.* xliv. 6.

O Lord, assist me through the fight;
My drooping spirit raise;
Make me triumphant in Thy might,
And Thine shall be the praise.

NOON :—

"A wise man is strong; yea, a man of knowledge increaseth strength."—*Prov.* xxiv. 5.

Oh, let not this world's scorching glow,
Thy Spirit's quickening dew efface;
Nor blast of sin too rudely blow,
And quench the trembling flame of grace.

EVENING :—

If enfeebled by age, have I not a special promise?—(*Isa.* xlvi. 4.)

In early years Thou wast my Guide,
And of my youth the Friend;
And, as my days began with Thee,
With Thee my days shall end.

SEPTEMBER 6.

MORNING:—

"I have inclined my heart to perform Thy statutes alway, even unto the end."—*Psa.* cxix. 112.

> Let no delusion make me stray,
> A wanderer from Thy blessed way;
> Nor, in the slippery paths of youth,
> Divert me from the God of truth.

NOON:—

"He giveth power to the faint."—*Isa.* xl. 29.

> When we cleave to earthly things,
>   Send Thy reviving grace;
> Raise our souls, and give them wings
>   To reach Thy holy place.

EVENING:—

Am I forsaking Christ, or cleaving to Him?—(*Acts* xi. 23.)

> Pressing onwards as we can
>   Still to this our life shall tend,
> Where FAITH's earliest steps began,
>   May life's latest moments end.

SEPTEMBER 7.

MORNING :—

"What I do, that I will do."—
2 *Cor.* xi. 12.

> Let us make the promise sure,
> Let us to the end endure,
> In the Saviour's love abiding,
> In the Saviour's strength confiding.

NOON :—

"The hoary head is a crown of glory, if it be found in the way of righteousness."—*Prov.* xvi. 31.

> If age steal o'er me, and decay
> My yielding form invade,
> The sooner 'twill be cast away
> . For one that cannot fade.

EVENING :—

The things that I purpose, do I purpose according to the flesh? (2 *Cor.* i. 17.)

> Oh, still restore our wandering feet
> And still direct our way,
> Till worlds shall fail, and faith shall greet
> The dawn of endless day.

SEPTEMBER 8.

Morning:—

"I will yet be more vile than thus."
—2 *Sam.* vi. 22.

Let the vain world pronounce it shame,
And fling their scandal on His cause,
We come to boast our Saviour's name,
And make our triumph in His cross.

Noon:—

"The slothful man saith, There is a lion in the way."—*Prov.* xxvi. 13.

What, wearied out with half a life?
Scared with this smooth unbloody strife?
Think where thy coward hopes had flown
Had Heaven held out a martyr's crown!

Evening:—

Am I conformed to the world?—
(*Rom.* xii. 2.)

Saviour, if of Zion's city
  I through grace a member am,
Let the world deride or pity,
  I will glory in Thy name.

SEPTEMBER 9.

MORNING:—

"The son of my vows!"—*Prov.* xxxi. 2.

> Poor worms of earth, for help we cry,
>   For grace to guide what grace has given;
> We ask for wisdom from on high,
>   To train our infant up for heaven.

NOON:—

"A wise son maketh a glad father."—*Prov.* xv. 20.

> Happy the home where Jesus' name
>   Is sweet to every ear;
> Where children early lisp His fame,
>   And parents hold Him dear.

EVENING:—

Do I teach my children the fear of God?—(1 *Chron.* xxviii. 9.)

> Regard the mother's anxious tears,
>   Her heart's desire, her earnest prayer;
> And while her infant charge she rears,
>   Crown with success her Christian care.

SEPTEMBER 10.

MORNING:—

"As long as he liveth he shall be lent to the Lord."—1 *Sam.* i. 28.

> Lent to us for a season, we
> Lend back our child, O Lord, to Thee;
> Assured, that if to Thee he live,
> We gain in what we seem to give.

NOON:—

"Train up a child in the way he should go."—*Prov.* xxii. 6.

> Oh, say not, dream not, heavenly notes
>   To childish ears are vain,
> That the young mind at random floats,
>   And cannot reach the strain.

EVENING:—

Do I turn teachings into prayers for my children?—(1 *Chron.* xxix. 19.)

> When we shall quit this mortal stage,
>   And all our work on earth be done,
> Give us to meet them in the skies,
>   To dwell for ever near Thy throne.

SEPTEMBER 11.

MORNING :—

"Thus saith thy son,...I will nourish thee."—*Gen.* xlv. 9—11.

Happy the man to whom He sends
Obedient children, faithful friends;
How sweet our daily comforts prove
When they are season'd with His love.

NOON :—

"The glory of children are their fathers."—*Prov.* xvii. 6.

In Thee our fathers put their trust;
Thy ways they humbly trod;
Honour'd and sacred is their dust,
And still they live to God.

EVENING :—

Do I care for my parents in their old age?—(*Prov.* xxiii. 22.)

Should o'er their path decline
The light of gladness, or of hope, or health,
Be Thou their solace, and their joy, and wealth,
As they have long been mine.

SEPTEMBER 12.

MORNING:—

"My voice shalt Thou hear in the morning, O Lord."—*Psa.* v. 3.

 Oh, lead me to Thy mercy-seat;
  Attract me nearer still;
 Draw me, like Mary, to Thy feet,
  To sit and learn Thy will.

NOON:—

"The fear of the Lord is the beginning of knowledge."—*Prov.* i. 7.

 To every doubt in Thee my heart
  An answer hopes to find;
 In every gladness, Lord, Thou art
  The deeper joy behind.

EVENING:—

Do I love private as well as public prayer?—(*Matt.* xiv. 23.)

 'Tis sweet to steal awhile away
  From every cumbering care,
 And spend the closing hours of day
  In humble grateful prayer.

SEPTEMBER 13.

MORNING :—

"In the day of my trouble I will call upon Thee."—*Psa.* lxxxvi. 7.

> Jesus, my sorrow lies too deep
>   For human sympathy;
> It knows not how to tell itself
>   To any but to Thee.

NOON :—

"The righteous shall never be removed."—*Prov.* x. 30.

> I need not fear my foes,
>   I need not yield to care,
> I need not sink beneath my woes,
>   For Thou wilt answer prayer.

EVENING :—

Do I watch for God's seasonable help?—(*Acts* xii. 6, 7.)

> Deliverance comes most bright and blest
>   At danger's darkest hour;
> And man's extremity is best
>   To prove almighty power.

SEPTEMBER 14.

MORNING :—

"I will wash mine hands in innocency ; so will I compass Thine altar, O Lord."—*Psa.* xxvi. 6.

> Since inward truth Thy laws require,
> That inward truth, O Lord, inspire ;
> Through all my soul let wisdom shine,
> And give me purity divine.

NOON :—

"How to perform that which is good, I find not."—*Rom.* vii. 18.

> Yet whilst Thy will we would pursue,
> Oft what we would we cannot do ;
> The sun may stand in zenith skies,
> But on the soul thick midnight lies !

EVENING :—

Am I schooling my heart to accept God's will ?—(*Psa.* cxxxi. 2.)

> Then when our hearts have ceased the troubled strife
> That frets, and fumes, and will not be content,
> A calmer joy will settle on our life,
> A peaceful welcome for what Thou hast sent.

SEPTEMBER 15.

Morning :—

"Come and let us join ourselves to the Lord in a perpetual covenant."— *Jer.* l. 5.

 Thine we are, for Thou hast made us;
  Thine, because redeem'd by Thee;
 Thine, for Thou hast ever led us;
  Thine we evermore would be.

Noon :—

"The grace of God...hath abounded. —*Rom.* v. 15.

 Where'er the greatest sins abound,
  By grace they are exceeded;
 Thy helping hand is always found
  With aid where aid is needed.

Evening :—

Am I obedient to conscience?— (2 *Tim.* i. 3.)

 Lord, cleanse this soul of mine,
  And all its powers renew;
 Give me to know Thy holy will,
  Thy holy will to do.

SEPTEMBER 16.

MORNING:—

"Come, and let us declare...the work of the Lord."—*Jer.* li. 10.

> The rebel soul that once withstood
> The Saviour's kindest call,
> Rejoices now, by grace subdued,
> To serve Him with her all.

NOON:—

"The Lord is good to all, and His tender mercies are over all His works."—*Psa.* cxlv. 9.

> May we love Thee, may we fear Thee;
> May Thy will, not ours, be done;
> Never leave us till we're near Thee
> In the home where all are one.

EVENING:—

Am I faithful to my vows?—(*Psa.* lxxvi. 11.)

> Not time, or place, or chance, or death, can bow
> My least desires unto the least remove,
> He firmly mine by oath, I His by vow,
> He mine by faith, and I am His by love.

SEPTEMBER 17.

MORNING :—

"We will wait upon Thee."—*Jer.* xiv. 22.

    Happy the man whose bliss supreme
      Flows from a source on high,
    And flows in one perpetual stream,
      When earthly springs are dry.

NOON :—

"In the day of prosperity be joyful; but in the day of adversity consider."—*Eccles.* vii. 14.

    Through every changing state of life,
      Each bright or clouded scene,
    Give us a meek and humbled mind,
      Contented and serene.

EVENING :—

Am I steadfast in my confidence?—(*Heb.* iii. 6.)

    Like those who watch for midnight's hour
      To hail the dawning morrow,
    I wait for Thee, I trust Thy power,
      Unmov'd by doubt or sorrow.

SEPTEMBER 18.

MORNING:—

"Christ is preached, and I therein do rejoice, yea, and will rejoice."—*Phil.* i. 18.

> Send, Lord, by whom Thou wilt,
>   The gospel of Thy Son,
> So but Thy glorious Church be built,
>   And precious souls be won.

NOON:—

"Be more ready to hear than to give the sacrifice of fools."—*Eccles.* v. 1.

> On Thee our hopes depend;
>   We gather round our Rock;
> Send whom Thou wilt, but condescend
>   Thyself to feed Thy flock.

EVENING:—

Do I pray for a blessing on the preached word?—(2 *Thess.* iii. 1.)

> Bid, bid Thy heralds publish loud
>   The blessings of Thy peaceful reign;
> And when they speak of sprinkling blood,
>   The mystery to the heart explain.

SEPTEMBER 19.

MORNING :—

"I will...set me upon the tower, and will watch to see what He will say."—*Hab.* ii. 1.

>With tearful eyes I look around;
> Life seems a dark and stormy sea;
>Yet midst the gloom I hear a sound,
> A heavenly whisper, "Come to Me."

NOON :—

"The eyes of a fool are in the ends of the earth."—*Prov.* xvii. 24.

>My soul, with all thy waken'd powers,
> Survey the heavenly prize;
>Nor let these glittering toys of earth
> Allure thy wandering eyes.

EVENING :—

Have I tasted that the Lord is good? —(*Psa.* xxxiv. 4, 8.)

>I came to Jesus as I was,
> Weary, and worn and sad,
>I found in Him a resting-place,
> And He has made me glad.

SEPTEMBER 20.

MORNING :—

"I cannot go beyond the word of the Lord."—*Numb.* xxii. 18.

> God hath said it, God hath said it,
>   God hath said, and I obey;
> God hath said it, God hath said it,
>   And with joy I go my way.

NOON :—

"I have hoped in Thy word."—*Psa.* cxix. 74.

> Hope thou in God, and He shall make
>   Thy path like noon-tide glow;
> Obey Him with a steadfast mind,
>   And Thou His smile shall know.

EVENING :—

Do I value ordinances as I find God in them?—(*Psa.* lxv. 4.)

> Nearer, yet nearer! oh, to be so near
> The great, good presence, that above all fear
> For this scene or the next my soul might move
> Beneath the shadow of that perfect love.

SEPTEMBER 21

MORNING:—

"Once have I spoken; but I will not answer."—*Job* xl. 5.

>I know that Thou art God,
>　And I would ever lie
>Submissive to Thy holy will,
>　Whate'er that will may be.

NOON:—

"Be still, and know that I am God."—*Psa.* xlvi. 10.

>He speaks, and all is still!
>　The swelling tumult hush'd!
>He smiles into the soul, and straight
>　Each murmuring thought is crush'd!

EVENING:—

Am I willing to endure the Refiner's fire?—(*Mal.* iii. 3.)

>I sit beside the furnace,
>　The gold will soon be pure,
>And blessed are those servants
>　Who to the end endure.

SEPTEMBER 22.

MORNING :—

"I will proceed no further."—*Job* xl. 5.

> I know Thy will is right,
>   Though it may seem severe;
> Thy path is still unsullied light,
>   Though dark it oft appear.

NOON :—

"God will bring thee into judgment."—*Eccles.* xi. 9.

> Father, forgive the heart that clings
>   Thus trembling to the things of time,
> And bid my soul on angel-wings
>   Ascend into a purer clime.

EVENING :—

Am I comforted concerning my dead?—(1 *Thess.* iv. 18.)

> Gaze not upon the narrow home
>   Of silence and despair;
> Oh, raise thy drooping eyes to heaven
>   And see an angel there.

SEPTEMBER 23.

Morning :—

"I shall go softly all my years in the bitterness of my soul."—*Isa.* xxxviii. 15.

Oh, wretched state of men,
The height of whose ambition is to borrow
  What must be paid again
With griping interest of the next day's sorrow.

Noon :—

"The rod and reproof give wisdom."—*Prov.* xxix. 15.

Lord, we expect to suffer here,
  Nor would we dare repine;
But give us still to find Thee near,
  And own us still for Thine.

Evening :—

Am I soothed by the sympathy of Christ?—(*Heb.* iv. 15.)

Oh, shame upon this listless heart
  So sad a sigh to heave,
As if thy Saviour had no part
  In thoughts that make thee grieve.

SEPTEMBER 24

Morning :—

"With my spirit within me will I seek Thee early."—*Isa.* xxvi. 9.

> In this valley of sorrow and strife
>   Prayer shall rise with my earliest breath,
> It shall mix in the business of life,
>   And soften the struggles of death.

Noon :—

"Whoso walketh wisely, he shall be delivered."—*Prov.* xxviii. 26.

> O Lord, amidst this mental night,
>   Amidst the clouds of dark dismay,
> Arise, arise, shed forth Thy light,
>   And kindle love's meridian day.

Evening :—

Do I trust my all to God's wisdom?—(2 *Sam.* xv. 25, 26.)

> In Thee I place my trust,
>   On Thee I calmly rest,
> I know Thee good, I know Thee just,
>   And count Thy choice the best.

SEPTEMBER 25.

Morning :—

"From the end of the earth will I cry unto Thee, when my heart is overwhelmed."—*Psa.* lxi. 2.

> Drooping mourner, canst thou languish
>   Near the great Consoler's feet?
> He can give thee joy for anguish:
>   Seek Him at the mercy-seat.

Noon :—

"God giveth...wisdom, and knowledge, and joy."—*Eccles.* ii. 26.

> The Lord of light, though veil'd awhile
>   He hides His noontide ray,
> Shall soon in lovelier beauty shine
>   To gild your closing day.

Evening :—

Do I know the love which casts out fear?—(1 *John* iv. 18.)

> Why should I shrink at Thy command,
>   Whose love forbid my fears,
> Or tremble at the gracious Hand
>   That wipes away my tears?

SEPTEMBER 26.

MORNING :—

"I will say,...Why hast Thou forgotten me?"—*Psa.* xlii. 9.

In all thy sufferings, think not, brother,
   Thine is a lone unfriended lot ;
Look up, and feel there is Another
   In sympathy who ceaseth not.

NOON :—

"The heart knoweth his own bitterness."—*Prov.* xiv. 10.

Only the Lord can hear,
   Only the Lord can see,
The struggle within, how dark and drear,
   Though calm the surface be.

EVENING :—

Do I stay my heart on the faithful love of Christ?—(*Eph.* v. 25—27.)

One Friend alone is changeless,
   The One too oft forgot,
Whose love hath stood for ages ;—
   Our Jesus changeth not !

SEPTEMBER 27.

MORNING :—

"Then shall the Lord be my God."
—*Gen.* xxviii. 20, 21.

> Lord, in the strength of grace,
> With a glad heart and free,
> Myself, my residue of days,
> I consecrate to Thee.

NOON :—

"The preparation of the heart in man...is from the Lord." *Prov.* xvi. 1.

> Lord; turn the stream of nature's tide;
> Let all our actions tend
> To Thee, their source; Thy love the guide,
> Thy glory be their end.

EVENING :—

Do I think heartless prayer will prevail?—(*James* iv. 3.)

> Lord, I often ask amiss;
> Lord, search my heart, and see;
> My motives purify, nor cease
> To draw my soul to Thee.

SEPTEMBER 28.

MORNING:—

"Thou art my God, I will exalt Thee."—*Psa*. cxviii. 28.

> Be all my heart, be all my days,
> Devoted to Thy single praise;
> And let my glad obedience prove
> How much I owe, how much I love.

NOON:—

"He is...my father's God, and I will exalt Him."—*Exod*. xv. 2.

> Our vows, our prayers, we now present
>   Before Thy throne of grace:
> God of our Fathers, be the God
>   Of their succeeding race.

EVENING:—

Do I think my parents' piety will suffice for me?—(*Ezek*. xviii. 4.)

> Come, let us share without delay
>   The covenant of His grace,
> Nor shall the years of distant life
>   Its memory e'er efface.

SEPTEMBER 29.

Morning :—

"I will sing unto the Lord, for He hath triumphed gloriously."—*Exod.* xv. 1.

> Earth to heaven, and heaven to earth,
> Tell His wonders, sing His worth;
> Age to age, and shore to shore,
> Praise Him, praise Him evermore.

Noon :—

"He loveth him that followeth after righteousness."—*Prov.* xv. 9.

> Yield to the Lord with simple heart
> All that thou hast, and all thou art;
> Renounce all strength but strength divine,
> And peace shall be for ever thine.

Evening :—

Do I expect to escape suffering?—(*Acts* xiv. 22.)

> What! was the promise made to thee alone,
> Art thou the excepted one?
> An heir of glory, without grief or pain?
> Oh, vision false and vain!

SEPTEMBER 30.

MORNING:—

"I must by all means keep this feast."—*Acts* xviii. 21.

> Be known to us in breaking bread,
>   But do not then depart;
> Saviour, abide with us, and spread
>   Thy table in our heart.

NOON:—

"Ye do show the Lord's death TILL HE COME."—1 *Cor.* xi. 26.

Feast after feast thus comes and passes by;
  Yet, passing, points to the great feast above,
Giving sweet foretastes of the festal joy,
  The Lamb's great bridal feast of bliss and love.

EVENING:—

Do I long for the vintage of Canaan?—(*Josh.* v. 12.)

> There is one land which knows no change,
>   Whose sun is ever high,
> But 'tis far beyond the cloudy range,
>   And above the starry sky.

OCTOBER 1.

MORNING :—

"I will take the cup of salvation, and call upon the name of the Lord." —*Psa.* cxvi. 13.

> Thy body broken for my sake,
>   My bread from heaven shall be;
> Thy testamental cup I'll take,
>   And thus remember Thee.

NOON :—

"The Lamb...shall feed them."— *Rev.* vii. 17.

> There is a scene where Jesus ne'er,
>   Ne'er leaves his happy guests;
> He spreads a ceaseless banquet there,
>   And love still fires their breasts.

EVENING :—

Does heavenly hope quicken me to earthly duty?—(2 *Cor.* v. 6—9.)

> I love by faith to take a view
>   Of brighter scenes in heaven;
> Such prospects oft my strength renew,
>   While here by tempests driven.

OCTOBER 2.

Morning :—

"The disciples...determined to send relief unto the brethren."—*Acts* xi. 29.

 Among the saints on earth
  Let mutual love be found,
 Heirs of the same inheritance,
  With mutual blessings crown'd.

Noon :—

"Show ye...the proof of your love."
—2 *Cor.* viii. 24.

Work if ye will; sow, reap, and gather in
 A full rich harvest, an abundant store;
Then open wide the hand to give again,
 And men shall bless you now and evermore.

Evening :—

Am I liberal in proportion to my means?—(*Luke* xxi. 3, 4.)

 Didst Thou for us, Lord, stoop so low
 That Thou did'st heaven itself forego,
 And shall we not ourselves deny
 The poor to feed, their wants supply?

OCTOBER 3.

MORNING:—

"This will I do."—*Luke* xii. 18.

Oh, righteous doom, that they who make
  Pleasure their only end,
Ordering the whole life for its sake,
  Miss that whereto they tend.

NOON:—

"In all labour there is profit."—*Prov.* xiv. 23.

The thorn, harsh emblem of the curse,
  Puts forth a paradise of flowers;
Labour, man's punishment, is nurse
  To halcyon joys at sunset hours.

EVENING:—

Has labour prepared me for rest?—
(*Eccles.* v. 12.)

O Lord, who by Thy presence hast made light
  The heat and burden of the toilsome day,
Be with me also in the silent night,
  Be with me now the daylight fades away.

OCTOBER 4.

MORNING :—

"I will meditate in Thy precepts, and have respect unto Thy ways."—*Psa.* cxix. 15.

Should all the forms that men devise
    Assault my faith with treacherous art,
I'd call them vanity and lies,
    And bind the gospel to my heart.

NOON :—

"The talk of the lips tendeth only to penury."—*Prov.* xiv. 23.

Change is hopefully begun
When something is in heart-truth done;
Musing only, all is dark;
Act, and you will strike a spark.

EVENING :—

Am I always planning, never acting?—(*Prov.* xxi. 25.)

Waste not so much time in weighing
    When and where thou shalt begin;
Too much thinking is delaying,
    And rivets but the chains of sin.

OCTOBER 5.

Morning :—

"I will meditate also of all Thy work, and talk of Thy doings."—*Psa.* lxxvii. 12.

   Evil and good before Thee stand,
     Thy mission to perform;
   The blessing comes at Thy command,—
     At Thy command the storm.

Noon :—

"Whom the Lord loveth, He correcteth."—*Prov.* iii. 12.

     So there is naught of anger
       In this my Father's stroke;
     He is but gently teaching
       My neck to bear the yoke.

Evening :—

Am I always repining, never rejoicing?—(2 *Cor.* vi. 10.)

     Often the clouds of deepest wo
       A sweet love-message bear;
     Dark though they seem, we cannot find
       A frown of anger there.

OCTOBER 6.

MORNING:—

"I will praise Thee;...Thine anger is turned away, and Thou comfortedst me."—*Isa.* xii. 1.

> When Mercy points where Jesus bleeds,
>   And Faith beholds Thine anger cease,
> And Hope to black despair succeeds,
>   This, Father, this alone is peace.

NOON:—

"God now accepteth thy works."—*Eccles.* ix. 7.

> Praise His name who died to save us;
>   'Tis by Him His people live;
> And in Him the Father gave us
>   All that boundless love could give.

EVENING:—

Is sin a burden heavier than I can weigh?—(*Psa.* xxxviii. 4.)

> But Thou, in spite of our offences past
>   And those, alas! which still in us are found,
> Hast lov'd us, Jesus, with a love so vast,
>   No span can reach it, and no plummet sound.

OCTOBER 7.

Morning:—

"I will delight myself in Thy statutes."—*Psa.* cxix. 16.

> Light is the yoke that, lined with love,
>   The willing neck confines,
> When ready feet obedient move
>   As He who rules inclines.

Noon:—

"They shall sing in the ways of the Lord."—*Psa.* cxxxviii. 5.

> Away with our sorrow and fear!
>   We soon shall recover our home,
> The city of saints shall appear,
>   The day of eternity come.

Evening:—

Is my helplessness a sorrow to me?—(*Rom.* vii. 24.)

> When harassed by ten thousand foes
>   Our helplessness we feel,
> Oh, give the weary soul repose,
>   The wounded spirit heal.

OCTOBER 8.

Morning:—

"My lips shall greatly rejoice when I sing unto Thee."—*Psa.* lxxi. 23.

>Open, Lord, mine inward ear,
>　And bid my heart rejoice;
>Bid my quiet spirit hear
>　Thy comfortable voice.

Noon:—

"Ye shall receive a crown of glory that fadeth not away."—1 *Pet.* v. 4.

>With joy may we our course pursue,
>And keep the crown of life in view,
>That crown which in an hour repays
>The labour of ten thousand days.

Evening:—

Do I willingly abide in Doubting Castle?—(*James* i. 6, 7.)

>Why should my soul indulge complaints,
>　And yield to dark despair?
>The meanest of my Father's saints
>　Are safe beneath His care.

OCTOBER 9.

MORNING:—

"He is my defence; I shall not be moved."—*Psa*. lxii. 6.

He lives! my bright and morning Star,
  To guide me through this howling waste;
My Sun, to warm my drooping heart;
  My Shield, to guard my anxious breast.

NOON:—

"He is a buckler to them that walk uprightly."—*Prov*. ii. 7.

Our shield, when sorrows round us press;
Our shield, when doubts and fears distress;
Our shield, when waves of trouble roll
And overwhelm the trembling soul.

EVENING:—

Have I this day found God my Shield and my Reward?—(*Gen*. xv. 1.)

When once the heavenly shores we gain,
Where we with Christ shall ever reign,
We'll praise and bless our faithful God,
No more our Shield, but our Reward.

OCTOBER 10.

MORNING :—

"Because of His strength will I wait upon Thee; for God is my defence."—*Psa.* lix. 9.

Sometimes my courage fails me,
　My strength seems well nigh gone;
But still Thy grace avails me,
　Thy strength still helps me on.

NOON :—

"So I prayed to the God of heaven."—*Neh.* ii. 4.

When at mid-day my task I ply,
With labouring hand or watchful eye,
I need the timely aid of prayer
To guard my soul from worldly care.

EVENING :—

Have I this day made David's God my trust?—(1 *Sam.* xxx. 6.)

And now the day is closing,
And night her gloomy shadow flings,
Let us lie down beneath Thy wings,
　With childlike trust reposing.

OCTOBER 11.

MORNING :—

"I will not be afraid of ten thousands of people that have set themselves against me round about."—*Psa.* iii. 6.

Amidst ten thousand snares I stand,
Upheld and guarded by Thy hand;
Thy words my fainting soul revive,
And keep my dying faith alive.

NOON :—

"This God is our God for ever and ever."—*Psa.* xlviii. 14.

Help me, Lord, in patience, now
  My spirit to possess;
Then, in Thy presence, may I know
  How fully Thou canst bless.

EVENING :—

Have I this day found Israel's God my Guide?—(*Exod.* xiii. 21, 22.)

Servant of God, hope on!
  Through tempests and through tears
The pillar of His presence see,
  Lighting the waste of years.

OCTOBER 12.

MORNING:—

"It is in mine heart to make a covenant with the Lord God of Israel."—
2 *Chron.* xxix. 10.

>Sacred to Thee alone,
> Be all these powers of mine,
>Then in the noblest sense my own,
> When most entirely Thine.

NOON:—

" Thou hast avouched the Lord this day to be thy God."—*Deut.* xxvi. 17.

>Yes, I'm Thine, I'm Thine for ever;
> Thee I'd love, and I'd obey;
>Be my King as well as Saviour,—
> Rule my heart with sovereign sway.

EVENING:—

Have I an assured hope that God is mine?—(*Psa.* xxxv. 3.)

>Mine! what rays of glory bright
> Now upon the promise shine!
>I have found the Lord my light!
> I am His and He is mine!

OCTOBER 13.

MORNING:—

"Till I die, I will not remove mine integrity from me."—*Job* xxvii. 5.

> The even paths of holiness,
> The straight highway I'll take,
> Unswerving in all truthfulness,
> For Thy great glory's sake.

NOON:—

"By the fear of the Lord men depart from evil."—*Prov.* xvi. 6.

> Great Author of each perfect gift,
> Thy sovereign grace display,
> That these rebellious roving powers
> May hearken and obey.

EVENING:—

Am I going on from strength to strength?—(*Psa.* lxxxiv. 7.)

> When age advances may we grow
> In faith, and hope, and love,
> And walk in holiness below
> To holiness above.

OCTOBER 14.

MORNING :—

"Truly my words shall not be false."
—*Job* xxxvi. 4.

Thou God of truth, for whom we long,
  Thou, who wilt hear our prayer,
Do Thine own battle in our HEARTS,
  And slay the falsehood THERE.

NOON :—

"It was impossible for God to lie."
—*Heb*. vi. 13—18.

His truth to Jacob shall prevail,
His oath to Abram cannot fail,—
The hope of saints in ancient days,
Which ages yet unborn shall praise.

EVENING :—

Are God's words as unstable as my ways?—(2 *Tim*. ii. 13.)

Oh, let me then at length be taught
  What I am still so slow to learn,
That God is love, and changes not,
  Nor knows the shadow of a turn.

OCTOBER 15.

MORNING:—

"We will remember the name of the Lord our God."—*Psa.* xx. 7.

> Inspired by Thee, our feeble souls
> Shall press victorious on,
> As the first dawning light improves
> To all the blaze of noon.

NOON:—

"Help us, O Lord our God, for we rest on Thee."—2 *Chron.* xiv. 11.

> The Christian's life is a weary strife,
> And often his heart would yield,
> But there's One to stand at his right hand
> His wavering faith to shield.

EVENING:—

Am I carnally or spiritually minded?—(*Rom.* viii. 5, 6.)

> 'Mid cares, and hopes, and pleasures mean,
> With eager fondness sought,
> Say, has one glance at things unseen
> Sublimed my earthly thought?

OCTOBER 16.

Morning:—

"We will go up, for the Lord hath delivered them into our hand."—1 *Sam.* xiv. 10.

From strength to strength go on,
  Wrestle, and fight, and pray,
Tread all the powers of darkness down,
  And win the well-fought day.

Noon:—

"The God of peace shall bruise Satan under your feet shortly."—*Rom.* xvi. 20.

Jehovah, by His ceaseless care,
  Whose eye can never sleep,
From earthly foes, from Satan's snare,
  My soul shall safely keep.

Evening:—

Have I this day yielded to the tempter?—(1 *John* i. 9.)

Oh, think not of my doubts and fears,
  My strivings with Thy grace divine;
Think upon Jesu's woes and tears,
  And let His merits stand for mine.

OCTOBER 17.

MORNING :—

"In God we boast all the day long."
—*Psa.* xliv. 8.

> He lives, the mighty Conqueror lives,
>   To tread my foes beneath His feet;
> I smile to see their failing power,
>   And triumph in their last defeat.

NOON :—

"The race is not to the swift, nor the battle to the strong, neither yet bread to the wise."—*Eccles.* ix. 11.

> Fond mortals but themselves beguile
>   When on themselves they rest;
> Blind is their wisdom, vain their toil,
>   By Thee, O Lord, unbless'd.

EVENING :—

Do I check self-glory by g'orying in God ?—(*Jer.* ix. 23, 24.)

> Perish each thought of human pride;
> Let God alone be magnified;
> His glory let the heavens resound,
> Shouted from earth's remotest bound.

OCTOBER 18.

MORNING :—

"I will show thee that I have yet to speak on God's behalf."—*Job* xxxvi. 2.

> At times a single voice hath power
>   To speed the cause of right;
> And earnest words, from earnest hearts,
>   Come wing'd with sovereign might.

NOON :—

"The heart of the wise teacheth his mouth."—*Prov.* xvi. 23.

> Be ours the bliss in wisdom's way
>   To guide untutor'd youth,
> And lead the mind that went astray
>   To virtue and to truth.

EVENING :—

Where do I cast the crown of success?—(*Rev.* iv. 10.)

> Should e'er Thy wonder-working grace
>   Triumph by our weak arm,
> Let not our sinful fancy trace
>   Aught human in the charm.

OCTOBER 19.

Morning :—

"I must work the works of Him that sent me."—*John* ix. 4.

Work while the daylight lasteth,
  Ere the shades of night come on,
Ere the Lord of the vineyard cometh,
  And the labourer's work is done.

Noon :—

"The night cometh, when no man can work."—*Ibid.*

Oh, teach me the celestial skill,
  Each solemn warning to improve;
And, while my days are shortening still,
  Prepare me for the joys above.

Evening :—

Am I weary *of* work, or only weary *in* work?—(*John* iv. 6, *comp.* 32—34.)

There is no night in heaven!
  In that blest world above,
Work never can bring weariness,
  And work itself is love.

OCTOBER 20.

MORNING:—

"He will prosper us; therefore we His servants will arise and build."—*Neh.* ii. 20.

> Did we not raise our hands to Thee,
>   Our hands might toil in vain;
> Small joy success itself would be,
>   If Thou Thy love restrain.

NOON:—

"The people had a mind to work."—*Neh.* iv. 6.

> Their works will with their faith increase,
>   And with their works their joys abound;
> Sweet is their hope, divine their peace,
>   And blessings all their steps surround.

EVENING:—

While willing to work, am I longing to depart?—(*Phil.* i. 23, 24.)

> 'Tis gloom and darkness here,
>   'Tis light and joy above;
> There all is pure, and all is clear,
>   There all is peace and love.

OCTOBER 21.

Morning :—

"Open Thou my lips, and my mouth shall show forth Thy praise."—*Psa.* li. 15.

    Upon the willows long
      My harp has silent hung;
    How should I sing a cheerful song
      Till Thou inspire my tongue?

Noon :—

"Worthy is the Lamb that was slain."—*Rev.* v. 12.

    Brightness of the Father's glory,
      Shall Thy praise unutter'd lie?
    Break, my tongue, such guilty silence;
      Sing the Lord who came to die.

Evening :—

Does my soul truly pant after God? —(*Psa.* xlii. 2.)

    Let me be with Thee where Thou art,
      My Saviour, my eternal Rest;
    Then only will this longing heart
      Be fully and for ever bless'd.

OCTOBER 22.

MORNING:—

"I will sing praises to the God of Jacob."—*Psa.* lxxv. 9.

> The God of Abraham praise,
> Who reigns enthroned above,
> Ancient of everlasting days,
> And God of love.

NOON:—

"They joy before thee according to the joy in harvest."—*Isa.* ix. 3.

> O Christ, be Thou our present joy,
> Our future great reward;
> Our only glory may it be
> To glory in the Lord.

EVENING:—

Do I know Christ as the Sun of Righteousness?—(*Mal.* iv. 2.)

> His presence, felt, enhances joy;
> His love can stop each flowing tear,
> And cause upon the darkest cloud
> The bow of mercy to appear.

OCTOBER 23.

MORNING:—

"In God will I praise His word."—*Psa.* lvi. 4, 10.

Firm are the words His prophets give,
Sweet words on which His children live;
Each of them is the voice of God,
Who spake, and spread the skies abroad.

NOON:—

"Let my mouth be filled with Thy praise and with Thine honour all the day."—*Psa.* lxxi. 8.

Thy presence only can bestow
Delights which never cloy;
Be this my solace here below,
And my eternal joy.

EVENING:—

Is Christ my all and in all?—(*Eph.* i. 22, 23.)

Lord, be my Safety and Defence,
My Light, my Joy, my Bliss;
My portion in the world to come,
My confidence in this.

OCTOBER 2

MORNING :—

"I will be no judge of such matters."
—*Acts* xviii. 15.

Not different food, not different dress,
  Compose the kingdom of our Lord;
But peace, and joy, and righteousness,
  Faith, and obedience to His word.

NOON :—

"Avoid foolish questions." *Tit.* iii. 9.

Not for a favourite form or name,
  But for immortal souls we care;
Bless, Saviour, our Jerusalem,
  That millions may her blessings share.

EVENING :—

Is it only through indolence I eschew controversy?—(2 *Tim.* ii. 15, 16.)

Jesus, Thou living Word,
  Speak to this soul of mine,
Make there Thy whisper to be heard,
  And teach me truth divine.

OCTOBER 25.

Morning :—

"I have kept myself from being burdensome unto you; and so will I keep myself."—2 *Cor.* xi. 9.

> Great things are not what I desire,
> Nor dainty meat, nor rich attire ;
> Content with little would I be,
> If, Lord, that little come from Thee.

Noon :—

"Before honour is humility." *Prov.* xv. 33.

> I charge my thoughts, be humble still,
>   And all my carriage mild,
> Content, my Father, with Thy will,
>   And quiet as a child.

Evening :—

Am I proud of my fancied humility ?—(*Gal.* vi. 3.)

> Oh, set me free by Thine own might
>   From pride, that subtlest form of sin ;
> And smite it, oft as in the fight
>   It rears its hydra head within.

OCTOBER 26.

MORNING :—

"Let us...follow after the things which make for peace."—*Rom.* xiv. 19.

Come as the Dove, and spread Thy wings,
   The wings of peaceful love,
And let Thy Church on earth become
   Blest, as the Church above.

NOON :—

"Hatred stirreth up strifes, but love covereth all sins."—*Prov.* x. 12.

Make all disharmony and strife
   Within Thine earthly fold to cease,
And grant to all the Church of Christ
   The fellowship of truth and peace.

EVENING :—

Do I indulge in anger and strife?—(*James* iii. 14—18.)

The Spirit like a peaceful dove,
   Flies from the realms of noise and strife,
Why should we vex and grieve His love,
   Who seals our souls to heavenly life?

OCTOBER 27.

Morning:—

"Behold, I will pray unto the Lord your God."—*Jer.* xlii. 4.

Soul of our souls, and Safeguard of the world,
Sustain (Thou only canst!) the sick of heart;
Restore their languid spirits; and recall
Their lost affections unto Thee and Thine.

Noon:—

"They are the enemies of the cross of Christ."—*Phil.* iii. 18.

 Let us not with selfish coldness
  See the sinner go astray;
 But with Moses' holy boldness,
  Plead and wrestle, weep and pray.

Evening:—

Do I plead with God for the unconverted?—(*Isa.* li. 9, 10.)

 Art Thou not still the same, O God,
  The same to hear, the same to save,
 As when Thy servant moved his rod
  At Thy command, and cleft the wave?

OCTOBER 28.

MORNING:—

"I determined not to know anything among you save Jesus Christ, and Him crucified."—1 *Cor.* ii. 2.

> Unfurl the blood-stain'd banner free,
>   To float above thee far and wide;
> And let thy watchword ever be,
>   In good or ill, "Christ crucified."

NOON:—

"He became obedient unto death."—*Phil.* ii. 8.

> In the cross of Christ I glory,
>   Towering o'er the wrecks of time;
> All the light of sacred story
>   Gathers round its head sublime.

EVENING:—

Do I pray for the growth of Christ's kingdom?—(*Psa.* lxxii. 15.)

> For Him shall prayer unceasing,
>   And daily vows ascend,
> His kingdom still increasing,
>   A kingdom without end.

OCTOBER 29.

MORNING:—

"I will speak of Thy testimonies."
—*Psa.* cxix. 46.

> Here consecrated water flows
>   To quench my thirst of sin;
> Here the fair tree of knowledge grows,
>   Nor danger dwells therein.

NOON:—

"In the wilderness shall waters break out, and streams in the desert."
—*Isa.* xxxv. 6.

> There is a stream whose gentle flow
>   Supplies the city of our God;
> Life, love, and joy, still gliding through,
>   And watering our divine abode.

EVENING:—

Do I pray for the spread of God's word?—(*Hab.* ii. 14.)

> Flow on, sweet stream, more largely flow,
>   The earth with glory fill;
> Flow on, till all the Saviour know,
>   And all obey His will.

OCTOBER 30.

MORNING:—

"As for me and my house, we will serve the Lord."—*Josh.* xxiv. 15.

> Where'er our dwelling shall be found,
> We will Thy throne of grace surround;
> An altar to Thy name we'll raise,
> With sacrifice of prayer and praise.

NOON:—

"Turn not to the right hand, nor to the left."—*Prov.* iv. 27.

> What well-advised ear regards
>   What earth can say?
> Her words are gold, but her rewards
>   Are painted clay!

EVENING:—

Do I render to God a "reasonable" service?—(*Rom.* xii. 1.)

> O Lord, henceforward let it be
> My whole desire to follow Thee,
> To glory in my Saviour's cross,
> And all beside to count as dross.

OCTOBER 31.

MORNING:—

"Nay, but we WILL serve the Lord."—*Josh.* xxiv. 21.

Now must we fight, if we would reign;
  Increase our courage, Lord;
We'll bear the toil, endure the pain,
  Supported by Thy word.

NOON:—

"Receive my instruction, and not silver; and knowledge rather than choice gold."—*Prov.* viii. 10.

Still let us, gracious Lord,
  Sit loose to all below;
And, to Thy love restored,
  No other portion know.

EVENING:—

Do I render to God a loving service?
—(2 *Cor.* viii. 12.)

Now to my Saviour I would live,
  To Him who for my ransom died;
Nor could untainted Eden give
  Such bliss as blossoms at His side.

NOVEMBER 1.

MORNING :—

"Whether it be good, or whether it be evil, we will obey."—*Jer.* xlii. 6.

What seemeth best, O Lord, to Thee,
  That must be truly blest;
And may it still seem good to me
  To follow Thy behest.

NOON :—

"Ye dissembled in your hearts ;... ye have not obeyed."—*Jer.* xlii. 20, 21.

Easy indeed it were to reach
  A mansion in the courts above,
If swelling words and fluent speech
  Might serve instead of faith and love.

EVENING :—

Am I one with Christ?—(*John* xvii. 21.)

Oh! make me, gracious Saviour, one with Thee,
  As ever one with very God Thou art;
  Dwell now and always throned within my heart,
And crown'd in heaven let me hereafter be.

NOVEMBER 2.

MORNING:—

"Save me, and I shall keep Thy testimonies."—*Psa.* cxix. 146.

> Dear Saviour, sweetly bind me
> Fast to Thy wounded side;
> And evermore remind me
> That Thou for me hast died.

NOON:—

"The Lord hath made all things for Himself."—*Prov.* xvi. 4.

> Dependent on Thy bounteous breath,
> We seek Thy grace alone,
> In childhood, manhood, age, and death,
> To keep us still Thine own.

EVENING:—

Do I own the God of creation?—(*Job* xxxvi. 24.)

> There's not a plant or flower below
> But makes Thy glories known;
> And clouds arise, and tempests blow,
> By order from Thy throne.

NOVEMBER 3.

Morning :—

"I will be glad and rejoice in Thee; I will sing praise to Thy name."—*Psa.* ix 2.

> Speak, Lord, and bid celestial peace
>   Relieve my aching heart;
> Oh, smile, and bid my sorrows cease,
>   And all my gloom depart.

Noon :—

"Consider the work of God."—*Eccles.* vii. 13.

> Leave to His sovereign will
>   To choose and to command;
> With wonder fill'd thou then shalt own
>   How wise, how strong His hand.

Evening :—

Do I adore the God of providence? —(*Psa.* lxvi. 9.)

> If light attend the course I run,
>   'Tis He provides those rays;
> And 'tis His hand that hides my sun,
>   If darkness cloud my days.

NOVEMBER 4.

MORNING:—

"Because Thy lovingkindness is better than life, my lips shall praise Thee."—*Psa.* lxiii. 3.

> Where'er I look, my wondering eyes
> Unnumber'd blessings see;
> But what is life, with all its bliss,
> If once compared with Thee?

NOON:—

"How excellent is Thy lovingkindness, O God."—*Psa.* xxxvi. 7.

> Thy favour and love I prefer
> To life in its happiest hours,
> Possess'd of a Paradise here
> When mercy my spirit o'erpowers.

EVENING:—

Do I delight in the God of grace?—(*Psa.* xxx. 5.)

> Life, like a fountain rich and free,
> Springs from the presence of the Lord;
> And in Thy light our souls shall see
> The glories promised in Thy word.

NOVEMBER 5.

Morning:—

"Then will I teach transgressors Thy ways."—*Psa.* li. 12, 13.

> Not for ourselves, the light of grace
> Did'st Thou on us bestow,
> But for the world's benighted race,
> Thy darken'd house below.

Noon:—

"The redemption of their soul is precious."—*Psa.* xlix. 8.

> God, to reclaim it, did not spare
> His well-beloved Son;
> Jesus, to save it, deign'd to bear
> The sins of all in One.

Evening:—

Do I believe in the forgiveness of sins?—(*Eph.* i. 7.)

> O Lamb of God, still keep me
> Near to Thy wounded side,
> For only then in safety
> And peace I can abide.

NOVEMBER 6.

MORNING :—

"I shall abide and continue with you all for YOUR furtherance and joy of faith."—*Phil.* i. 25.

> If life be long, I will be glad,
>   That I may long obey;
> If short, yet why should I be sad
>   To soar to endless day?

NOON :—

"God requireth that which is past."—*Eccles.* iii. 15.

> Life is real, life is earnest,
>   And the grave is not its goal;
> "Dust thou art, to dust returnest,"
>   Was not spoken of the soul.

EVENING :—

Do I believe in the immortality of the soul?—(*Matt.* xxv. 46.)

> God is earnest; kneel and pray
> Ere thy season pass away;
> Ere He set His judgment throne;
> Ere the day of grace be gone.

NOVEMBER 7.

MORNING :—

"I will speak, that I may be refreshed."—*Job* xxxii. 20.

> May every heart confess Thy name,
>   And ever Thee adore,
> And, seeking Thee, itself inflame
>   To seek Thee more and more.

NOON :—

"Every idle word that men shall speak, they shall give account thereof."—*Matt.* xii. 36.

> God of pureness, God of grace,
> Let not idle words have place;
> But, to check their heedless flow,
> Watchful earnestness bestow.

EVENING :—

Do I make known the atoning Christ to perishing sinners?—(*Acts* xiii. 38.)

> Give tongues of fire, and hearts of love,
>   To preach the reconciling word;
> Give power and unction from above,
>   Whene'er the joyful sound is heard.

NOVEMBER 8.

MORNING:—

"When I come again I will repay thee."—*Luke* x. 35.

> The wicked borrows of his friends,
>   But ne'er designs to pay;
> The saint is merciful and lends,
>   Nor turns the poor away.

NOON:—

"He that walketh uprightly, walketh surely."—*Prov.* x. 9.

> Faint not, Christian; though the road,
> Leading to thy blest abode,
> Darksome be, and dangerous too,
> Christ, thy guide, shall bring thee through.

EVENING:—

Do I take daily account of my soul's stock?—(*Isa.* lvi. 10—12.)

> Do the work to-day appointed;
>   Shun all indolent delay;
> Draw not bills upon to-morrow;
>   Pay the dues of life to-day.

NOVEMBER 9.

MORNING:—

"As we have...opportunity, let us do good unto all men."—*Gal.* vi. 10.

> Mercy through Jesus we have found,
> Free mercy from above;
> May mercy move us to fulfil
> The perfect law of love.

NOON:—

"The liberal soul shall be made fat."—*Prov.* xi. 25.

> Ah! not to self, ah! not to self,
> Let thinking souls devote their powers;
> But, spurning folly, ease, and pelf,
> For God and man employ their hours.

EVENING:—

Do I practice daily kindnesses?—(*Gen.* xl. 6, 7.)

> Did I this day for small or great,
> My own pursuits forego,
> To lighten by a feather's weight
> The mass of human wo?

NOVEMBER 10.

MORNING:—

"Take us the foxes, the little foxes, that spoil the vines."—*S. Song* ii. 15.

> Against each evil, great or small,
>   Oh, may I watch and pray;
> And from the faintest shades of sin,
>   Indignant, turn away.

NOON:—

"The beginning of strife is as when one letteth out water." *Prov.* xvii. 14.

> Oh, that my tender soul might fly
>   The first approach of ill,
> Quick as the apple of the eye
>   Sin's slightest touch to feel.

EVENING:—

Am I holy in little things?—(*Luke* xvi. 10.)

> Teach me, my God and King,
>   In all things Thee to see;
> And what I do in anything
>   To do it as for Thee.

NOVEMBER 11.

MORNING:—

"My soul shall be joyful in the Lord."—*Psa.* xxxv. 9.

What shall I do my God to love,
 My loving God to praise,
The length and breadth and height to prove
 And depth, of sovereign grace!

NOON:—

"Thy faithfulness is unto all generations."—*Psa.* cxix. 90.

Thy mercies how tender,
 How firm to the end,
Our Maker, Defender,
 Redeemer, and Friend.

EVENING:—

Am I heeding the flight of time?—(*Psa.* xc. 5, 9, 10.)

Time speeds away, away, away,
Another hour, another day,
Another month, another year,
Drop from us as the leaflets sear.

NOVEMBER 12.

Morning :—

"I will offer in His tabernacles sacrifices of joy."—*Psa.* xxvii. 6.

> There in Thy truth will I rejoice,
> And hymn Thy goodness in my lays;
> And mind, and heart, and soul, and voice,
> Shall join to magnify Thy praise.

Noon :—

"Thou, O Lord, art in the midst of us."—*Jer.* xiv. 9.

> And art Thou my Father above?
> Will Jesus abide in my heart?
> Oh, bind me so fast with Thy love,
> That I never from Thee shall depart.

Evening :—

Am I improving each moment?— (*Eph.* v. 16.)

> The moments in their fleetness
> Are flowers of rich perfume;
> Waste not their precious sweetness,
> While yet for thee they bloom.

NOVEMBER 13.

MORNING :—

"I will go unto the altar of God, unto God my exceeding joy."—*Psa.* xliii. 4.

> Oh, that I could now adore Him
>   Like the heavenly host above,
> Who for ever bow before Him,
>   And unceasing praise His love.

NOON :—

"In Thy favour our horn shall be exalted."—*Psa.* lxxxix. 17.

> Saviour of souls, while I from Thee
>   A single smile obtain,
> Though destitute of all things else,
>   I'll glory in my gain.

EVENING :—

Am I wise for eternity?—(*Prov.* xxiii. 15, 19.)

> Oh, haste! at Jesu's call be wise;
>   The precious time redeem;
> Nor everlasting joys despise
>   For what is but a dream.

NOVEMBER 14.

MORNING:—

"I will not take anything that is thine, lest thou shouldest say, I have made Abram rich."—*Gen*. xiv. 23.

> I would not change my blest estate
> For all the world calls good or great;
> And while my faith can keep her hold,
> I envy not the sinner's gold.

NOON:—

"For your sakes He became poor."
—2 *Cor*. viii. 9.

> The manger was His infant bed;
> His home the mountain cave;
> He had not where to lay His head;
> He borrow'd e'en His grave.

EVENING:—

Is mine the prayer of Agur?—(*Prov.* xxx. 7—9.)

> While worldly men with all their store
> Are ever grasping after more,
> With Agur's wish content I'll live,
> Nor grude them aught this earth can give.

NOVEMBER 15.

MORNING:—

"I will not go."—*Neh.* vi. 11.

Great is their peace who love Thy law;
    How firm their souls abide;
Nor can a bold temptation draw
    Their steady feet aside.

NOON:—

"Ponder the path of thy feet."—*Prov.* iv. 26.

I am lost without Thy ray;
    Guide my wandering footsteps, Lord;
Light my dark and erring way
    By the noontide of Thy word.

EVENING:—

Is mine the purity of Joseph?—(*Gen.* xxxix. 9.)

Lord, Thou hast search'd and seen me through;
Thine eye commands with piercing view
My rising and my resting hours,
My heart and flesh with all their powers.

NOVEMBER 16.

MORNING:—

"My lips shall not speak wickedness."—*Job* xxvii. 4.

 If secret fraud should dwell
  Within this heart of mine,
 Purge out, O God, that cursed leaven,
  And make me wholly thine!

NOON:—

"The Lord hearkened and heard."—*Mal.* iii. 16.

 ..... Beneath our eaves,
Each sound His watchful ear receives;
Hush idle words, and thoughts of ill!
Your Lord is listening; peace, be still!

EVENING:—

Is mine the guilelessness of Nathaniel?—(*John* i. 47.)

 Am I an Israelite indeed,
  Without a false disguise?
 Have I renounced my sins? and left
  My refuges of lies?

NOVEMBER 17.

Morning:—

"Hear me, O Lord; I will keep Thy statutes."—*Psa.* cxix. 145.

> I ask a godly fear,
>   A quick discerning eye,
> That looks to Thee when sin is near,
>   And sees the tempter fly.

Noon:—

"He that hearkeneth unto counsel is wise."—*Prov.* xii. 15.

> Draw, Holy Spirit, nearer,
>   And in our hearts abide;
> Oh, make our judgment clearer,
>   Our minds inform and guide.

Evening:—

Like the eunuch, do I welcome instruction?—(*Acts* viii. 31.)

> O ye His saints who taste His love,
>   And deeper mysteries know,
> Instruct my soul, and show my feet
>   The way I ought to go.

NOVEMBER 18.

Morning:—

"Give me understanding, and I shall keep Thy law."—*Psa.* cxix. 34.

> My God, accept my heart this day,
> And make it always Thine,
> That I from Thee no more may stray,
> No more from Thee decline.

Noon:—

"He was a faithful man, and feared God above many."—*Neh.* vii. 2.

> Attend, O Lord, my daily toil
> With blessings from above;
> Grant that my soul may watchful be,
> And full of faith and love.

Evening:—

Like Laodicea, am I lukewarm?— (*Rev.* iii. 15, 16.)

> As Thou hast died for me,
> Oh, may my love to Thee,
> Pure, warm, and changeless be,—
> A living fire!

NOVEMBER 19.

MORNING:—

"My hands will I lift up unto Thy commandments, which I have loved."—*Psa.* cxix. 48.

Oh, let Thy grace within me reign;
Each word, and act, and thought restrain,
Save such as aid me to fulfil
The sacred precepts of Thy will.

NOON:—

"It is joy to the just to do judgment."—*Prov.* xxi. 15.

To see the law by Christ fulfilled,
   And hear His pardoning voice,
Changes a slave into a child,
   And duty into choice.

EVENING:—

Like Peter, do I follow afar off?—(*Mark* xiv. 54.)

Walk in the light, and thou shalt find
   Thy heart made truly His,
Who dwells in cloudless light enshrined,
   In whom no darkness is.

NOVEMBER 20.

MORNING:—

"Of myself I will not glory, but in mine infirmities."—2 *Cor.* xii. 5.

> Bless and sanctify this cross;
> Pity and relieve my pain;
> And convert the present loss
> Into everlasting gain.

NOON:—

"The righteous...and their works are in the hand of God."—*Eccles.* ix. 1.

> The wintry winds are round our way,
> The light of heaven is dim;
> Yet One there is who bids us stay
> Our fainting hearts on Him.

EVENING:—

Do I love much, because much forgiven?—(*Luke* vii. 47.)

> Ah, grace! into unlikeliest hearts
> It is thy boast to come;
> The glory of thy light to find
> In darkest spots a home.

NOVEMBER 21.

MORNING :—

"In the shadow of Thy wings will I rejoice."—*Psa.* lxiii. 7.

> Lord, Thou art precious to my heart,
>   My portion and my joy;
> For ever let Thy boundless grace
>   My warmest thoughts employ.

NOON :—

"Thine expectation shall not be cut off."—*Prov.* xxiii. 18.

> Though thy sky be over-clouded,
>   Though thy path be dark and drear,
> Though thy soul with doubt be shrouded,
>   Oh, let Faith still conquer Fear.

EVENING :—

Have I resignation, or only submission?—(*Job* ii. 10.)

> Renew my will from day to day;
> Blend it with Thine, and take away
> All that now makes it hard to say,
>   "Thy will be done!"

NOVEMBER 22.

Morning:—

"So shall I talk of Thy wondrous works."—*Psa.* cxix. 27.

> How gracious and how wise
>   Is our chastising God;
> And, oh! how rich the blessings are
>   Which blossom from His rod.

Noon:—

"Treasures of wickedness profit nothing."—*Prov.* x. 2.

> Whate'er consists not with Thy love,
>   Oh, teach me to resign;
> I'm rich, to all the intents of bliss,
>   If Thou, O God, art mine.

Evening:—

Do I covet holiness by "any" means?—(*Phil.* iii. 11.)

> I would press closer to Thee,
>   A heavier cross to bear,
> So I might better know Thee,
>   And more Thy Spirit share.

NOVEMBER 29.

MORNING:—

"I will remember the works of the Lord."—*Psa.* lxxvii. 11.

Care shall not come across my breast;
  He clothes the grass, and shall I need?
Doubts shall no more my peace molest,
  Since He who made, vouchsafes to feed.

NOON:—

"In the fear of the Lord is strong confidence."—*Prov.* xiv. 26.

When waves of sorrow round me swell,
  My soul is not dismayed;
I hear a voice I know full well,
  "'Tis I, be not afraid!"

EVENING:—

Have I accepted the calls of mercy?—(*Jer.* xxxiii. 3.)

  At Thy gracious invitation,
    I approach Thy throne divine;
  Visit me with Thy salvation;
    Gently tell me Thou art mine.

NOVEMBER 24.

MORNING:—

"Open to me the gates of righteousness; I will go into them, and praise the Lord."—*Psa.* cxviii. 19.

> Thou child of man, rejoice!
> The Righteous One hath died!
> Behold by faith thy seals of love,
> His hands, His feet, His side.

NOON:—

"My times are in Thy hand."—*Psa.* xxxi. 15.

> Times of sickness and of health;
> Times of penury and wealth;
> Times of trial and of grief;
> Times of triumph and relief.

EVENING:—

Have I accepted Christ, and Christ alone?—(*Acts* iv. 12.)

> Christ alone! Christ alone!
> Echo back, my soul, the words!
> Thy redeeming Saviour crown,
> King of kings, and Lord of lords.

NOVEMBER 25.

MORNING :—

"I will mention the lovingkindnesses of the Lord."—*Isa.* lxiii. 7.

> Thy mercy tempers every blast
> To them that seek Thy face,
> And mingles with the tempest's roar
> The whispers of Thy grace.

NOON :—

"God hath set the one over against the other."—*Eccles.* vii. 14.

> The fragrance of the rose is lent
> Thy homeward path to cheer;
> The thorn to make thee more intent
> On the thornless amaranth there.

EVENING :—

Am I living for Christ, and Christ only?—(*Rom.* xiv. 9.)

> Oh, may my single aim be now
> To live in Him that died,
> And nought on earth desire or know
> But Jesus crucified.

NOVEMBER 26.

MORNING :—

"I will praise Thee, O Lord, among the people."—*Psa.* lvii. 9.

> Sing with glad anticipation!
> Mortals and immortals sing!
> Jesus comes with full salvation;
> Jesus doth His glory bring.

NOON :—

"He saved others; Himself He cannot save."—*Matt.* xxvii. 42.

> Oh! wonderful the wonders left undone,
> And scarce less wonderful than those He wrought! [thought,
> Oh! self-restraint passing all human
> To have all power, and be as having none!

EVENING :—

Is mine an experimental religion?—(*Rom.* v. 2—5.)

> Jesus, mine Advocate above,
> Let me not hear of Thee alone,
> But make the wonders of Thy love
> By deep experience sweetly known.

NOVEMBER 27.

MORNING:—

"I will declare Thy greatness."—
Psa. cxlv. 6.

> May my constant study be,
> While I live, to live to Thee;
> Let it be my steady aim
> Still to glorify Thy name.

NOON:—

"We have an Advocate with the Father, Jesus Christ the righteous."—
1 *John* ii. 1.

> He ever lives to intercede
>   Before His Father's face;
> Give Him, my soul, thy cause to plead,
>   Nor doubt the Father's grace.

EVENING:—

Is my practice at variance with my profession?—(*Ezek.* xxxiii. 31.)

> But, oh! my God, tho' grovelling I appear
> Upon the ground, and have a rooting here
> Which hales me downward, yet in my desire
> To that which is above me I aspire.

NOVEMBER 28.

MORNING:—

"My lips shall utter praise, when Thou hast taught me Thy statutes."—*Psa.* cxix. 171.

My grateful soul shall speak His praise
  Who turns its tremblings into songs;
And those who mourn shall learn from me
  Salvation to our God belongs.

NOON:—

"The Father Himself loveth you."—*John* xvi. 27.

In busy mart and crowded street,
No less than in the still retreat,
Thou, Lord, art near our souls to bless
With all a parent's tenderness.

EVENING:—

Do I endure as seeing the Invisible?—(*Heb.* xi. 27.)

Thou art near; yes, Lord, I feel it;
  Thou art near, where'er I move;
And though sense would fain conceal it,
  Faith oft whispers it in love.

NOVEMBER 29.

MORNING :—

"Come ye, and let us walk in the light of the Lord."—*Isa.* ii. 5.

> O Sun of Righteousness, arise,
> And guide us on our way
> To yon fair mansions in the skies
> Of joyous, cloudless day.

NOON :—

"Thou shalt walk in thy way safely."—*Prov.* iii. 23.

> The pilgrim-path of trial
> We do not fear to view;
> We know His voice who calls us,
> We know Him to be true.

EVENING :—

Amid earthly darkness, have I light?—(1 *John* i. 4, 5.)

> When mystery clouds our darken'd path,
> We'll check our dread, our doubts reprove;
> In this our soul sweet comfort hath,
> That Thou art Love!

NOVEMBER 30.

MORNING :—

"God is...a very present help in trouble; therefore will not we fear."
—*Psa.* xlvi. 1—3.

Had I a glance of Thee, my God,
　Kingdoms and men would vanish soon,
Vanish, as though I saw them not,
　As a dim candle dies at noon.

NOON :—

"We have...an house not made with hands."—2 *Cor.* v. 1.

Our everlasting hopes arise
Above the ruinable skies,
Where the Eternal Builder reigns,
And His own court His power maintains.

EVENING :—

Amid earthly storms, am I fearless?
—(*Isa.* xliii. 1, 2.)

Calm as the summer's ocean, we
Can all the wreck of nature see,
While grace secures us an abode,
Unshaken as the throne of God.

DECEMBER 1.

MORNING:—

"Our heart shall rejoice in Him."
—*Psa.* xxxiii. 21.

When anxious cares would break my rest,
And grief would tear my throbbing breast,
Thy tuneful praises, raised on high,
Shall check the murmur and the sigh.

NOON:—

"God, Thy God, hath anointed Thee with the oil of gladness."—*Psa.* xlv. 7.

Hail, fount of blessings, hail! In Thee
Our life, our strength, our all we see!
While in Thy God Thy joys endure,
In Thee our blessings rest secure!

EVENING:—

Amid earthly losses, have I hold on Christ?—(*Rom.* viii. 35.)

Lord, 'tis enough! Thy voice we hear;
  The crown by faith we see;
No sorrows shall o'erwhelm our souls,
  Since none divide from Thee.

DECEMBER 2.

MORNING:—

"Whereto we have already attained, let us walk by the same rule."—*Phil.* iii. 16.

> Hold out, O fainting soul, hold out,
> Though fierce the fight, and long;
> The palm-wreath shall be thine at last;
> Look upward, and be strong..

NOON:—

"The slothful hideth his hand in his bosom."—*Prov.* xxvi. 15.

> Why should my heart descend so low
> To brood on earth, a world of woe,
> While heaven, where endless pleasures roll,
> Waits to entrance my new-born soul!

EVENING:—

Am I tempted as was Peter?— (*Luke* xxii. 31, 32.)

> When Satan, by my sins made bold,
> Strives from Thy cross to loose my hold,
> Then with Thy pitying arms enfold;
> And plead, oh! plead for me.

DECEMBER 3.

MORNING :—

"Let us not be weary in well-doing."—*Gal.* vi. 9.

> Sow, when the morning breaketh
>   In beauty o'er the land;
> And when the evening falleth,
>   Withhold not thou thy hand.

NOON :—

"They that sow in tears shall reap in joy."—*Psa.* cxxvi. 5.

> Yonder in joy the sheaves we bring
>   Whose seed was sown on earth in tears;
> There, in our Father's house, we sing
>   The song too sweet for mortal ears.

EVENING :—

Like Rachel, do I refuse to be comforted?—(*Jer.* xxxi. 15.)

> Be not weary, weeping Christian!
>   Tears endure but for the night;
> Joy, deep joy, thy spirit greeting,
>   Will return with morning's light.

DECEMBER 4.

MORNING :—

"We cannot but speak the things we have seen."—*Acts* iv. 20.

 Oh, help us, Lord, to tell
  The mercy we have found,
 E'en as the blossom's dew-filled bell
  Sheds its sweet odour round.

NOON :—

"As one whom his mother comforteth, so will I comfort you."—*Isa.* lxvi. 13.

 May the Lord our hearts impress,
  Make them like His own above,
 Fill'd with all the tenderness
  And all the strength of love.

EVENING :—

Am I known of God, as was Abraham?—(*Gen.* xviii. 19.)

 On me Thou hast bestow'd Thy grace;
  Be to my children kind;
 Among Thy saints give THEM a place;
  And leave not one behind.

DECEMBER 6.

MORNING:—

"I will praise Thee, for I am fearfully and wonderfully made."—*Psa.* cxxxix. 14.

    For all the blessings of creation,
    For daily life and renovation,
  As well as for the great redemption,
      Thee, Lord, I praise.

NOON:—

"O visit me with Thy salvation."—*Psa.* cvi. 4.

  When once Thou visitest the heart,
    Then truth begins to shine,
  Then earthly vanities depart,
    Then kindles love divine.

EVENING:—

Have I set my face Zionward?—(*Jer.* l. 5.)

  Have I renounced my former love
    Of earth and earthly toys?
  Have I a glimpse of heaven above?
    A taste for holy joys?

DECEMBER 6.

Morning :—

"I will have respect unto Thy statutes continually."—*Psa.* cxix. 117.

Call to thy God for grace to keep
Thy vows; and if thou break them, weep.
Weep for thy broken vows, and vow again;
Vows made with tears cannot be still in vain.

Noon :—

"Pay that which thou hast vowed."
—*Eccles.* v. 4.

Searcher of hearts, to Thee is known
The frailty which I humbly own;
How poor, how feeble is my will,
When I Thy precepts would fulfil.

Evening :—

Am I resolutely going on my way?
—(2 *Pet.* ii. 21.)

Let the road be rough and dreary,
And its end far out of sight,
Foot it bravely, strong or weary,
Trust in God, and do the right.

DECEMBER 7.

MORNING:—

"My words shall be of the uprightness of my heart."—*Job* xxxiii. 3.

Search, Lord, oh! search my inmost heart;
Thy light, and hope, and joy impart;
From guilt and error set me free,
And guide me safe to heaven and Thee.

NOON:—

"The upright shall have good things in possession."—*Prov.* xxviii. 10.

What though we roam the wide world o'er
  And have no earthly treasure?
Our Father's love can give us more
  Than words of wealth can measure.

EVENING:—

Am I happy as a pilgrim should be?
—(*Isa.* xxxv. 8—10.)

  Cease, ye pilgrims, cease to mourn;
    Press onward to the prize;
  Soon your Saviour will return
    Triumphant in the skies.

DECEMBER 8.

MORNING:—

"I will praise Thy name, for Thou hast done wonderful things."—*Isa.* xxv. 1.

>Lift up to God the voice of praise,
>   Whose goodness, passing thought,
>Loads every minute, as it flies,
>   With benefits unsought.

NOON:—

"Hope maketh not ashamed."—*Rom.* v. 5.

>Hope hath a harvest in the spring;
>In winter doth of summer sing;
>Feeds on the fruits while blossoming,
>   Yet nips no bloom.

EVENING:—

Have I been this day to Calvary?—(*Mark* xv. 25—39.)

>Sweet the moments, rich in blessing,
>   Which before the Cross I spend,
>Life, and health, and peace possessing,
>   From the sinner's dying Friend.

DECEMBER 9.

MORNING:—

"I will be glad and rejoice in Thy mercy."—*Psa.* xxxi. 7.

> I'll celebrate Thy glory
>   With all Thy saints above,
> And tell the joyful story
>   Of Thy redeeming love.

NOON:—

"Let the righteous be glad."—*Psa.* lxviii. 3.

> Come, shout aloud the Father's grace,
>   The Saviour's dying love;
> Soon you shall sing the glorious theme
>   In loftier strains above.

EVENING:—

Do I love the mount of communion? —(*Matt.* xvii. 4.)

> Away, ye dreams of mortal joy!
> Raptures divine my thoughts employ!
> I see the King of glory shine,
> And feel His love, and call Him mine!

DECEMBER 10.

MORNING :—

" I will rejoice in Thy salvation."—
Psa. ix. 14.

Of all the crowns Jehovah wears,
   Salvation is His dearest claim ;
That gracious sound, well-pleased, He hears;
   And owns Emmanuel for His name.

NOON :—

" In Thy name shall they rejoice all the day."—*Psa.* lxxxix. 16.

[They] carry music in their heart
Through dusky lane and wrangling mart,
Plying their daily task with busier feet,
Because their secret souls a holy strain repeat.

EVENING :—

Do I often ascend the hill Pisgah ?
—(*Deut.* xxxiv. 1—3.)

Of Canaan's land, from Pisgah's top
   May I but have a view,
Though Jordan should o'erflow its banks,
   I'll boldly venture through.

DECEMBER 11.

MORNING :—

"I said, I will be wise."—*Eccles.* vii. 23.

> To fear Thy power, to trust Thy grace,
>   Is our divinest skill;
> And he the wisest of our race
>   That best obeys Thy will.

NOON :—

"Fools die for want of wisdom."—*Prov.* x. 21.

> We barter life for pottage, sell true bliss
>   For wealth or power, pleasure or renown;
> Then, Esau-like, our Father's blessing miss,
>   And wash with fruitless tears our faded crown.

EVENING :—

How long have I yet to live?—(*Psa.* xc. 12.)

> Great Source of wisdom, teach my heart
>   To know the price of every hour,
> That time may bear me on to joys
>   Beyond its measure and its power.

DECEMBER 12.

MORNING :—

"Mine eyes are EVER toward the Lord."—*Psa*. xxv. 15.

Oh, hallow'd be the approaching day,
Let meekness be our morning ray,
And faithful love our noonday light,
And hope our sunset calm and bright.

NOON :—

"Look unto Me, and be ye saved."
—*Isa*. xlv. 22.

My eyes and my desire
 Are ever to the Lord;
I love to plead His promises,
 And rest upon His word.

EVENING :—

How am I kept from day to day?—
(1 *Pet*. i. 5.)

Saints by the power of God are kept
 Till the salvation come;
We walk by faith as strangers here,
 Till Christ shall call us home.

DECEMBER 13.

MORNING:—

"Of all that Thou shalt give me, I will surely give the tenth unto Thee."—*Gen.* xxviii. 22.

> To Thee, as our covenant-God,
> We'll our whole selves resign,
> And count that not our tenth alone,
> But all we have is Thine.

NOON:—

"My son, give Me thine heart."—*Prov.* xxiii. 26.

> Jesus, my Lord, how rich Thy grace!
> Thy beauties, how complete!
> How shall I count the matchless sum?
> How pay the mighty debt?

EVENING:—

How much do I owe my Lord?—(2 *Cor.* ix. 15.)

> The love I owe for sin forgiven,
> For power to believe,
> For present peace, and promised heaven,
> No angel can conceive!

DECEMBER 14.

MORNING :—

"I press toward the mark for the prize of the high calling."—*Phil.* iii. 14.

"Heavenward, heavenward!" only this
　Is my watchword on the earth,
For the love of heavenly bliss,
　Counting all things little worth.

NOON :—

"This one thing I do."—*Phil.* iii. 13.

Lord, HELP me this one thing to do,
To keep the glorious prize in view;
Fain would I leave the things behind,
And heaven on earth in Jesus find.

EVENING :—

Do I count earthly gain as loss or Christ?—(*Phil.* iii. 7, 8.)

For Him I count as gain each loss,—
　Disgrace for Him, renown;
Well may I glory in His cross,
　While He prepares my crown.

DECEMBER 15.

Morning:—

"Neither count I my life dear unto myself, so that I might finish my course with joy."—*Acts.* xx. 24.

 So, whene'er in death I slumber,
  With the wise, let me rise,
 Counted in their number.

Noon:—

"All are of the dust, and all turn to dust again."—*Eccles.* iii. 20.

 Shortly this prison of my clay
  Must be dissolv'd and fall;
 Then, O my soul, with joy obey
  Thy heavenly Father's call.

Evening:—

Do I realize how near eternity I may be?—(1 *Sam.* xx. 3.)

One beating pulse, one feeble struggle o'er,
May open wide the everlasting door;
Yes! for that bliss unspeakable, unseen,
Is ready,—and the veil of flesh between
 A gentle sigh may rend!

DECEMBER 16.

Morning :—

"I will sing a new song unto Thee, O God."—*Psa.* cxliv. 9.

[In heaven], with all the blood-bought throng,
  From sin and sorrow free,
I'll sing the new eternal song
  Of Jesu's love to me.

Noon :—

"They sung a new song, saying, Thou art worthy."—*Rev.* v. 9.

Sing we the song of those who stand
  Around the eternal throne,
Of every kindred, clime, and land,
  A multitude unknown.

Evening :—

Does my heart raise its Hallelujahs? —(*Luke* xix. 40.)

Hallelujah! song of gladness,
  Song of everlasting joy!
Hallelujah! song the sweetest,
  That can angel-hosts employ!

DECEMBER 17.

MORNING:—

"I will praise Thee with uprightness of heart."—*Psa.* cxix. 7.

O for the living flame
  From His own altar brought,
To touch our lips, our minds inspire,
  And wing to heaven our thought.

NOON:—

"Wilt thou set thine eyes upon that which is not?"—*Prov.* xxiii. 5.

Teach me the flattering path to shun
In which the thoughtless many run,
Who for a shade the substance miss,
And grasp their ruin in their bliss.

EVENING:—

Is my name written in heaven?—
(*Luke* x. 20.)

Write but my name upon the roll
  Of the redeem'd above,
Then heart, and mind, and strength, and soul,
  I'll love Thee for Thy love.

DECEMBER 18.

MORNING :—

"I will sacrifice unto Thee with the voice of thanksgiving."—*Jonah* ii. 9.

There is a song so thrilling,
So far all songs excelling,
That they who sing it, sing it oft again,
So deep and earnest, yet so sweet and plain.

NOON :—

"A wise man will hear, and will increase learning."—*Prov.* i. 5.

'Tis but in part I know Thy will;
I bless Thee for the sight;
When will Thy love the rest reveal
In glory's clearer light?

EVENING :—

Is holiness a habit of my soul?—(1 *John* iii. 9.)

We work with silent industry,
Unconscious of the toil;
As of itself some goodly tree
Bears fruit in fertile soil.

DECEMBER 19.

MORNING :—

"My mouth shall praise Thee with joyful lips."—*Psa*. lxiii. 5.

> Lord, in Thy love I yet behold
> An undiminish'd store,
> A depth unmeasured and untold,
> A sea without a shore.

NOON :—

"It is the glory of God to conceal a thing."—*Prov*. xxv. 2.

> I welcome all Thy sovereign will,
> For all that will is love;
> And when I know not what Thou dost,
> I wait the light above.

EVENING :—

Is my heart established with grace? —(*Heb*. xiii. 9.)

Come, fill our hearts with inward strength;
  Make our enlarged souls possess,
And learn the height, and breadth, and length,
  Of Thine unmeasurable grace.

DECEMBER 20.

MORNING :—

"I determined this with myself, that I would not come again to you in heaviness."—2 *Cor.* ii. 1.

> But feeble my compassion proves,
> And can but weep where most it loves;
> Thine own all-saving arm employ,
> And turn these drops of grief to joy.

NOON :—

"Heaviness in the heart of man maketh it stoop."—*Prov.* xii. 25.

> Let no false comfort lift us up
>   To confidence that's vain;
> Nor let their faith and courage droop
>   Who love the Lamb once slain.

EVENING :—

Do I lament where I ought to labour?—(*Josh.* vii. 10.)

> Up and toil with all thy might;
> Noon is fading into night;
> Like the ever-moving wave,
> We are rushing to the grave.

DECEMBER 21.

MORNING:—

"I will sing of mercy and judgment."
—*Psa.* ci. 1.

God of my life! how good, how wise,
  Thy judgments to my soul have been!
They were but mercies in disguise,
  The painful remedies of sin.

NOON:—

"Who can make that straight which He hath made crooked?"—*Eccles.* vii. 13.

The songs of everlasting years
  That mercy shall attend,
Which leads thro' sufferings of an hour,
  To joys that never end.

EVENING:—

Do I weep where I ought to sing?
—(*John* xx. 13, 14.)

Why all these unbelieving fears?
  Jehovah's arm is strong!
Oh, chide the sighs, and groans, and tears,
  And turn them to a song.

DECEMBER 22.

MORNING:—

"I will give thanks unto Thee for ever."—*Psa.* xxx. 12.

> I cannot, Lord, Thy purpose see;
> Yet all is well, since ruled by Thee.

NOON:—

"Thou shalt be like a watered garden."—*Isa.* lviii. 11.

> A blessing such as this our hearts might reap
> Through the long day, and heavenly freshness keep,
> If, knowing how the day and the day's glare
> Must beat upon them, we would largely steep
> And water them betimes with dews of prayer.

EVENING:—

Do I diligently seek the Spirit's influences?—(*Luke* xi. 9—13.)

> Come, Thou best of all donations,
>   God can give, or we implore!
> Having Thy sweet consolations,
>   We can ask and wish no more.

DECEMBER 23.

MORNING:—

"We will walk in the name of the Lord our God for ever."—*Mic.* iv. 5.

> Weary and faint, by cares oppress'd,
>   We still are travelling on
> To that bright land of peace and rest,
>   Where our Forerunner's gone.

NOON:—

"I will not leave you comfortless."—*John* xiv. 18.

Come to me through life's changing way!—
And, when its pulses cease to play,
Then, Saviour, bid me come to Thee,
That where Thou art, I too may be.

EVENING:—

Do I bear the conflict in hope of conquest?—(*Rev.* iii. 21.)

> Soon, as Thou overcamest,
>   I too soon shall overcome,
> And bless the love which kept me
>   So long away from home.

DECEMBER 24.

MORNING :—

"Through God we shall do valiantly."
—*Psa.* lx. 12.

Now save us, Lord, from slavish fear,
   Now let our hopes be firm and strong,
Till Thy salvation shall appear,
   And joy and triumph raise the song.

NOON :—

"Behold, I come quickly."—*Rev.* xxii. 12.

The Lord of love, the Lord of might,
   The King of all created,
Shall back return to claim His right,
   On clouds of glory seated.

EVENING :—

Do I hopefully wait for Christ's appearing?—(*Tit.* ii. 13.)

The unbelieving world shall wail,
   While we rejoice to see the day;
Come, Lord, nor let Thy promise fail,
   Nor let Thy chariot long delay.

DECEMBER 25.

MORNING:—

"Let us now go even unto Bethlehem, and see this thing which is come to pass."—*Luke* ii. 15.

> Babe of Bethlehem, Lord of glory,
>   Prince of peace, Incarnate Word,
> Bless the hearts that now adore Thee
>   And proclaim Thee Christ the Lord.

NOON:—

"Glory to God in the highest, and on earth peace, goodwill toward men."—*Luke* ii. 14.

> This day rejoice, and sweetly sing!
> Voices, like bells of silver, ring!
> While lute and psalm with sweet delight
> The blessing of Christ's birth recite!

EVENING:—

Do I thankfully remember Christ's first advent?—(*Isa.* ix. 6.)

> Lo! He lays His glory by!
> Born, that man no more may die;
> Born, to raise the sons of earth;
> Born, to give them second birth.

DECEMBER 26.

Morning:—

"A froward heart shall depart from me."—*Psa.* ci. 4.

Uphold Thy servant through the day;
Direct my steps in wisdom's way;
Let me not walk where scorners walk,
And sinful men profanely talk.

Noon:—

"A faithful man who can find?"—*Prov.* xx. 6.

Thy very bride her portion
  And calling hath forgot,
And seeks for ease and glory
  Where Thou, her Lord, art not.

Evening:—

Am I prepared for the midnight cry?—(*Matt.* xxv. 6.)

Oh! call, Beloved; heavenly Bridegroom, call!
Am I not listening for the long-loved voice?
Oh! keep not silence! call, Beloved, call,
  And bid this longing heart at length rejoice.

DECEMBER 27.

MORNING:—

"I will hear what God the Lord will speak."—*Psa.* lxxxv. 8.

> O God, the listening ear impart
> To hear Thee tell Thy will,
> And then bestow the ready heart
> Thy statutes to fulfil.

NOON:—

"We are but of yesterday, and know nothing."—*Job* viii. 9.

> Minors are we of yesterday,
> Nor into manhood rise
> Till death pronounces us of age,
> And crowns us for the skies.

EVENING:—

Do I long for the "beatific vision?"—(1 *John* iii. 2.)

Draw, draw this fleshly curtain that denies
The gracious presence of Thy glorious eyes;—
Or give me faith, and by the eye of grace
I shall behold Thee, though not face to face.

DECEMBER 28.

Morning :—

"Whatsoever thing the Lord shall answer you, I will declare it."—*Jer.* xlii. 4.

Come, Lord; come Wisdom, Love, and Power;
   Open our ears to hear;
Let us not miss the accepted hour;
   Save, Lord, by love—or fear.

Noon :—

"Every word of God is pure."—*Prov.* xxx. 5.

   In vain shall Satan rage
     Against a book divine,
Where wrath and lightning guard the page,
    Where beams of mercy shine.

Evening :—

Do I seek the revival of grace?—(*Acts* iv. 31, 33.)

    Send the baptism of Thy Spirit,
     Shed the Pentecostal fire;
   Let us all Thy grace inherit;
     Waken—crown—each good desire.

DECEMBER 29.

MORNING :—

"I will endeavour that after my decease ye may have these things always in remembrance."—2 *Pet.* i. 15.

> Happy, if with my latest breath
> I may but speak His name,
> Preach Him to all, and cry in death,
> "Behold, behold the Lamb!"

NOON :—

"Blessed are the dead which die in the Lord."—*Rev.* xiv. 13.

> Mourn not the dead ;—'tis they alone
>   Who are the peaceful and the free!
> The purest olive-branch is known
>   To twine about the cypress-tree.

EVENING :—

Do I daily think of death?—(1 *Cor.* xv. 31.)

> Jesus lives! no longer now
>   Can thy terrors, Death, appal us;
> Jesus lives! and this we know,
>   Thou, O grave, canst not enthrall us.

DECEMBER 30.

MORNING :—

"As always, so now also, Christ shall be magnified in my body, whether it be by life or by death."—*Phil.* i. 20.

> In Thee I live, in Thee I die,
> Content, for Thou art ever nigh.

NOON :—

"'The righteous hath hope in his death."—*Prov.* xiv. 32.

> What is death?—To sleep in Jesus
> When this weary strife is o'er,
> And to sorrows, sins, diseases,
> Never to awaken more.

EVENING :—

Am I constantly and joyously living as within view of Jordan's waves?—(*Josh.* iii. 1.)

> Let them bear me away
> In His presence to be :
> 'Tis but seeing Him nearer,
> Whom always I see.

DECEMBER 31.

MORNING :—

"Into Thy hand I commit my spirit."—*Psa.* xxxi. 5.

> Oh, meet me in the valley,
>   When heart and flesh shall fail,
> And softly, safely lead me on,
>   Until within the veil.

NOON :—

"Thou crownest the year with Thy goodness."—*Psa.* lxv. 11.

> For Thy mercy and Thy grace
>   Faithful through another year,
> Hear our song of thankfulness !—
>   Father, Son, and Spirit, hear !

EVENING :—

Do I wish to die the death of the righteous?—(*Numb.* xxiii. 10.)

> Oh, for the death of those that die
>   Like daylight in the west,
> That sink in peace, like waves at eve,
>   To calm unbroken rest.

SPECIAL PRAYERS

IN

SCRIPTURE WORDS.

I.—A Sabbath Prayer.
II.—A Penitent's Prayer
III.—A Backslider's Prayer.
IV.—Prayer in Prosperity
V.—Prayer in Perplexity
VI.—Prayer in Sickness.
VII.—Prayer in Bereavement
VIII.—Prayer in Temptation.

SPECIAL PRAYERS.

I.—A SABBATH PRAYER.

Unto Thee lift I up mine eyes, O Thou that dwellest in the heavens. Prosper, I pray Thee, Thy servant this day. This is the day which the Lord hath made; remember me, O my God, for good. I have loved the habitation of Thy house. As the hart panteth after the water-brooks, so panteth my soul after Thee, O God; my soul thirsteth for God, for the living God, to see Thy power and Thy glory, so as I have seen Thee in the sanctuary. O send out Thy light and Thy truth; let them lead me; then will I go unto the altar of God, unto God my exceeding joy. I will wash mine hands in innocency; so will I compass Thine altar, O Lord; for Thou art not a God that hath pleasure in wickedness, neither shall evil dwell with Thee. Praise waiteth for Thee, O God, in Zion; O Thou that hearest prayer, unto Thee shall all flesh come. Thou, O God, hast prepared of Thy goodness for the poor. Let Thy priests be clothed with righteousness, and let Thy saints shout for joy. Open Thou mine eyes, that I may behold wondrous things out of Thy law. Open Thou my lips, and my mouth shall show forth Thy praise.

Blessed be the Lord God; and let the whole earth be filled with His glory. Amen.

SPECIAL PRAYERS.

II.—A PENITENT'S PRAYER.

BEHOLD, I am vile; what shall I answer Thee? I have gone astray like a lost sheep. Mine iniquities are gone over my head; as a heavy burden, they are too heavy for me. God be merciful to me a sinner. Make haste to help me, O Lord my salvation. Have mercy upon me, O God, according to Thy loving kindness; according unto the multitude of Thy tender mercies, blot out my transgressions. Remember not the sins of my youth, nor my transgressions: according to Thy mercy remember Thou me, for Thy goodness' sake, O Lord. For Thy name's sake, O Lord, pardon mine iniquity; for it is great. Wash me throughly from mine iniquity, and cleanse me from my sin. Wash me, and I shall be whiter than snow. Heal me, O Lord, and I shall be healed; save me, and I shall be saved; for I will declare mine iniquity, I will be sorry for my sin. I have sinned, and perverted that which was right, and it profited me not. I have borne chastisement, I will not offend any more. Create in me a clean heart, O God, and renew a right spirit within me. Show me Thy ways, O Lord; teach me Thy paths.

Hear the prayer of Thy servant, and cause Thy face to shine, for the Lord's sake. AMEN.

SPECIAL PRAYERS.

III.—A BACKSLIDER'S PRAYER.

O MY God, I am ashamed and blush to lift up my face to Thee. In me, that is, in my flesh, dwelleth no good thing. Who shall deliver me from the body of this death? Lord, all my desire is before Thee; and my groaning is not hid from Thee. Turn Thou me, and I shall be turned; for Thou art the Lord my God. Be not a terror unto me; Thou art my hope in the day of evil. Seek Thy servant; for I do not forget Thy commandments. Lord, Thou knowest all things; Thou knowest that I love Thee. Oh that I were as in months past, as in the days when God preserved me; for then was it better with me than now. My soul cleaveth unto the dust; quicken Thou me according to Thy word. Hide Thy face from my sins, and blot out all mine iniquities. Cast me not away from Thy presence, and take not Thy Holy Spirit from me. What have I to do any more with idols? Cleanse Thou me from secret faults: keep back Thy servant also from presumptuous sins. Restore unto me the joy of Thy salvation; and my tongue shall sing aloud of Thy righteousness.

Unto Him that loved us, and washed us from our sins in His own blood, be glory and dominion for ever and ever. AMEN.

SPECIAL PRAYERS.

IV.—PRAYER IN PROSPERITY.

Lord, who is like unto Thee! Thou art good, and doest good. Thou crownest the year with Thy goodness. The earth is full of Thy mercy. Thou hast set my foot in a large room; Thy gentleness hath made me great. Who am I, O Lord God, and what is my house, that Thou hast brought me hitherto? I am not worthy of the least of all Thy mercies, and of all the truth which Thou hast showed unto Thy servant. O continue Thy lovingkindness; and with Thy blessing let the house of Thy servant be blessed for ever. Show me a token for good. Turn away mine eyes from beholding vanity; and quicken Thou me in Thy way. Hold up my goings in Thy paths, that my footsteps slip not. Keep me as the apple of the eye, hide me under the shadow of Thy wings. Thou hast been my help; leave me not, neither forsake me, O God of my salvation. Redeem me, and be merciful unto me. Rejoice the soul of Thy servant.

Blessed be the Lord, for He hath showed me His marvellous kindness. Let the Lord be magnified, which hath pleasure in the prosperity of His servant. Unto the King eternal, immortal, invisible, be honour and glory for ever and ever. Amen.

SPECIAL PRAYERS.

V.—PRAYER IN PERPLEXITY.

HEAR my prayer, O Lord, and let my cry come unto Thee. In the day when I call, answer me speedily. My soul is full of troubles. I am come into deep waters, where the floods overflow me. I am ready to halt, and my sorrow is continually before me. Withhold not Thou Thy tender mercies from me, O Lord. Be pleased, O Lord, to deliver me; O Lord, make haste to help me. Thou hast delivered my soul from death; wilt Thou not deliver my feet from falling? I know not how to go out or come in; give therefore Thy servant an understanding heart. Lighten mine eyes, lest those that trouble me rejoice when I am moved. Send Thine hand from above. For Thy name's sake, lead me and guide me. Cause me to know the way wherein I should walk. Teach me to do Thy will. Make Thy way straight before my face. I am a stranger in the earth; hide not Thy commandments from me. Uphold me according unto Thy word, that I may live. Hold Thou me up, and I shall be safe. Order my steps in Thy word, and let not any iniquity have dominion over me.

To God only wise, be glory through Jesus Christ for ever. AMEN.

SPECIAL PRAYERS.

VI.—PRAYER IN SICKNESS.

O LORD, rebuke me not in Thy wrath, neither chasten me in Thy hot displeasure. Correct me, but with judgment; not in Thine anger, lest Thou bring me to nothing. Have mercy, O Lord; heal me, for my bones are vexed. I am feeble, and sore broken: my heart panteth, my strength faileth me. I am weary with my groaning. Lord, I am oppressed; undertake for me. Hear my prayer, O Lord; and give ear unto my cry; hold not Thy peace at my tears. Remove Thy stroke away from me. Remember how short my time is. O spare me, that I may recover strength before I go hence. The grave cannot celebrate Thee. Be merciful unto me, and raise me up. If it be possible, let this cup pass from me; nevertheless not as I will, but as Thou wilt. Lord, be merciful unto me, and heal my soul; for I have sinned. Look upon mine affliction and my pain; and forgive all my sins. Show me wherefore Thou contendest with me. Make me to know mine end, and the measure of my days. My times are in Thy hand. Into Thine hand I commit my spirit; for Thou hast redeemed me, O Lord God of truth;—

—Unto whom be honour and power everlasting. AMEN.

SPECIAL PRAYERS.

VII.—PRAYER IN BEREAVEMENT.

OUT of the depths have I cried unto Thee, O Lord. Let my prayer come before Thee; incline Thine ear unto my cry. The troubles of my heart are enlarged. The thing which I greatly feared is come upon me; and that which I was afraid of is come unto me. Lover and friend hast Thou put far from me, and mine acquaintance into darkness. I was dumb, I opened not my mouth, because Thou didst it. Thou turnest man to destruction, and sayest, "Return, ye children of men." Shall not the Judge of all the earth do right? The Lord gave, and the Lord hath taken away; blessed be the name of the Lord. Attend unto my cry, for I am brought very low; I am desolate and afflicted. But mine eyes are unto Thee, O God the Lord; in Thee is my trust; leave not my soul destitute. Though I walk in the midst of trouble, Thou wilt revive me. When my father and my mother forsake me, then the Lord will take me up. With Thee is the fountain of life. Thou shalt guide me with Thy counsel, and afterward receive me to glory.

Thanks be to God which giveth us the victory through our Lord Jesus Christ,—to whom be glory for ever and ever. AMEN.

SPECIAL PRAYERS.

VIII.—PRAYER IN TEMPTATION.

My God, my God, why hast Thou forsaken me? why art Thou so far from helping me? They be many that fight against me, O Thou Most High. Save me from the lions' mouth. The wicked have laid a snare for me. The proud have had me greatly in derision. All my familiars watched for my halting, saying, "Peradventure he will be enticed, and we shall prevail against him." By the words of Thy lips I have kept me from the paths of the destroyer. Hide me from the secret counsel of the wicked. Pull me out of the net that they have privily laid for me; for Thou art my strength. Incline not my heart to any evil thing. O keep my soul, and deliver me. Let integrity and uprightness preserve me. Let me not be ashamed. Let not mine enemies triumph over me. Let them not say in their hearts, "Ah! so would we have it." Say unto my soul, "I am thy salvation." Let those that fear Thee turn unto me, and those that have known Thy testimonies.

Thanks be unto God which always causeth us to triumph in Christ. To Him be glory and dominion for ever and ever. AMEN.

EXTRACTS

FROM

SUNSET THOUGHTS.*

1. ISAAC; or, Eventide.
2. LOT; or, Harvest-time.
3. METHUSELAH; or, Length of Days.
4. ELIZABETH; or, Holiness of Life.
5. DAVID; or, Old and Grey-headed.
6. DEBORAH; or, Old and Faithful.
7. CALEB; or, Aged and Vigorous.
8. BARZILLAI; or, Aged and Infirm.
9. JACOB; or, An Old Man's Memories.
10. PAUL; or, An Old Man's Hope.
11. ELI; or, Old Age Sorrowing.
12. SAMUEL or, Old Age Honoured.
13. ESTHER. or, Danger and Deliverance.
14. HANNAH; or, Prayer and Praise.
15. JOB; or, Life's Changes.
16. ABRAHAM; or, Life's Trials.
17. ASA; or, The Sick Bed.
18. JOHN; or, The Beloved Disciple.
19. LEMUEL'S MOTHER; or, A Queen's Advice.
20. LAPIDOTH'S WIFE; or, A Mother in Israel.
21. MATTHEW; or, The Saviour's Call.
22. PETER; or, Growth in Grace.
23. ANNA; or, Life's Waiting-time.
24. MOSES; or, Canaan in Sight.

---

* SUNSET THOUGHTS; or, Twenty-four Bible Narratives for the Aged. By the Author of "Daily Communion," "Bible Words for Daily Use," &c. Large type. Fcap. 8vo, 1s. 6d. cloth. Superior edition, on fine paper, crown 8vo, 2s. 6d. extra cloth.

Extracts from Sunset Thoughts;

ISAAC; or, Eventide.*

"So full of rich and varied beauty are the narratives given in the Bible, that we can never find reason to grow weary of them, though we study them all our life-time through.... Isaac went out to meditate. The margin reads it "to pray." We learn a good lesson here. Meditation and prayer ought to go together. When they do, they help each other. There are some men who pray, or try to pray, but they hardly ever meditate. It follows that prayer is with them hard, cold, heavy, dull. They have not counted up their mercies, and they know not what thanks to give. They have not searched their heart, and they know not what sins to confess. They have not thought over their wants, and they know not what blessings to ask.

"But there are some men who meditate, and do not pray. They think, but their thoughts do not lead them to God.... They find out their helplessness, but do not lay hold on the help that is in Christ. They feel the disease of sin, but keep away from the Great Physician. They pore over their griefs, but do not turn to the one true Comforter...."

---

* SUNSET THOUGHTS; or, Twenty-four Bible Narratives for the Aged. Large type (English). Fcap. 8vo, 1s. 6d. cloth. Superior edition, on fine paper, crown 8vo, 2s. 6d. extra cloth.

ELI; or, Old Age Sorrowing.*

"None who have looked at the well-known picture of old Eli and the youthful Samuel, are likely to forget the contrast which it shows. . . . What has been the cause of that old man's sorrow? . . . . He grieves not for the dead, but for the living; not for the happy dead, but for 'the living lost.' He had been too indulgent when his boys were young. He had seen them going wrong, and 'he restrained them not.' He had known of their selfish greediness, and 'he frowned not upon them.' He had been told of their plunging into the blackest crimes, and his intended reproof faltered into the tame and spiritless reproof, 'Why do ye such things? for I hear of your evil dealings by all this people?' . . . .

"Can it be that your case is like that of Eli? are you mourning over prodigals whom you left to themselves in their youth, and who are now bringing shame on their own heads and yours? You need not despair. If your sons will not listen to you, turn from them to God. . . . Pray for the blessing, if needful, as long as life shall last; and it may be that years after your head is laid low in the dust, the blessing will be given."

---

* SUNSET THOUGHTS; or, Twenty-four Bible Narratives for the Aged. Large type (English). Fcap. 8vo, 1s. 6d. cloth. Superior edition, on fine paper, crown 8vo, 2s. 6d. extra cloth.

Extracts from Sunset Thoughts;

DAVID; or, Old and Grey-headed.*

..... "Amid growing infirmities of the outward life, David's mind and soul remained bright and clear. It was from the experience of a life-time that he could say with confidence to Solomon his son, 'Be strong and of a good courage; fear not, nor be dismayed, for the Lord God, even my God, will be with thee; He will not fail thee, nor forsake thee.' .... When he wrote his last inspired words, he was looking forward to the Coming One, who was all his 'salvation' and all his 'desire,' even the Righteous One, who was to shine forth 'as the light of the morning when the sun riseth,' and as 'a morning without clouds.' When he uttered his last dying charge to Solomon, he could calmly say, 'I go the way of all the earth.' ...

"Am I old and grey-headed? then let me remember David's example, and utter David's prayer, and look up to David's God. I have no strength of my own, but, like David, 'I will go in the strength of the Lord God.' I have no righteousness worth the name, but, like David, 'I will make mention' of His, even of His only, who has become 'the Lord our righteousness.'"

---

* SUNSET THOUGHTS; or, Twenty-four Bible Narratives for the Aged. Large type, (English.) Fcap. 8vo, 1s. 6d. cloth. Superior edition, on fine paper, crown 8vo, 2s. 6d. extra cloth.

CALEB; or, Aged and Vigorous.*

"In Caleb's vigour and in his prosperity we see that sometimes even outwardly the righteous may 'bring forth fruit in their old age,' and may still be 'fat and flourishing.'... At seventy-five—at eighty-five—are you almost as strong and hearty as you were at forty? have years crept upon you unawares, and left little or no mark save on the bald or hoary head? is yours a bright old age, 'like the green winter of the holly tree?' Boast not of this your strength, but let thanks rise where thanks are due. It may be that you owe your present vigour in part to your own prudent and temperate habits. Yet recollect that no painstaking of yours would have availed, if God's help had been withdrawn. In spite of all your watchfulness, He might have cut you off at a stroke, or He might have withered you by blighting sickness. Do not presume upon your strength. Do not imagine that your health and vigour are to last for ever. When you were young, did you put away religious thought, as if old age would be a more convenient season? When grey hairs were upon you, did you still say 'Time enough yet?' How is it with you this day?"

---

* SUNSET THOUGHTS; or, Twenty-four Bible Narratives for the Aged. Large type (English). Fcap. 8vo, 1s. 6d. cloth. Superior edition, on fine paper, crown 8vo, 2s. 6d. extra cloth.

Extracts from Sunset Thoughts;

PAUL; or, An Old Man's Hope.*

.... "Was Paul building his hope of heaven on his own doings? Not so. The fight he had fought was a good fight, because it was fought under the banner of Christ, the Captain of his salvation. The course he had finished was one on which he first entered by renouncing for ever his own righteousness by the works of the law. The faith he had kept was that of which he said, 'I live by the faith of the Son of God, who loved me and gave Himself for me.' Had Paul for one moment placed his hopes of salvation on his own watchfulness, his own perseverance, his own steadfastness, he would at that moment have been forsaking the fight, declining the course, and ceasing to keep the faith. Now, as ever, his trust was in Christ alone. . . .

"If Paul's hope is not yet your's, how can you obtain it? By seeking his Lord and Master as your Saviour. The crown of life is for all who are Christ's. . . . The crown is given to them that 'love His appearing.' Those who love His appearing love Him; and those who love Him, have it in their hearts at least to fight the fight, and run the race, and keep the faith. . . ."

* Sunset Thoughts; or, Twenty-four Bible Narratives for the Aged. Large Type (English). Fcap. 8vo, 1s. 6d. cloth. Superior Edition, on fine paper, crown 8vo, 2s. 6d. extra. cloth.

Uniform with "DAILY BIBLE TEXT-BOOKS."

Royal 64mo, toned paper, cloth lettered, 6d.

OUR HOME ABOVE;
Or, Echoes from Canaan.

BY THE

AUTHOR OF "SUNSET THOUGHTS;
Or, Bible Narratives for the Aged."

"Oh, for the joy no eye hath seen,
No human heart hath known!
For faint and low
Fall the echoes below
Of the songs around His throne!"

"THE human heart instinctively craves a heaven of outward and inward bliss. Philosophers and poets in all ages have given voice to the question of the multitude, 'Where—or rather, What—is that radiant shore?' The inquiry is not unanswered. The songs of heaven awake echoes that have reached the earth; and the more finely attuned our spiritual sense, the more distinct will be our perception of those rich, sweet harmonies. It is well day by day to bend a listening ear, and catch an inspiration of joy and hope from those sounds of everlasting gladness.

"Thanks be to God, we have a heaven revealed. The revelation has been *gradual*. At first, an instance or two of translation thither, and a few

Our Home Above.

scattered hints of prophecy, but no more. Then life and immortality were brought to light in the gospel, when He who is the way to heaven, taught us its truth, and promised us its life. Next was given the Revealing Spirit, to enlighten us as to the riches of the glory of the inheritance. Even yet is the revelation only *partial*. Celestial glory is still 'a glory that shall be revealed.' We know enough to quicken intelligent hope; not enough to induce impatience of hope deferred."

The subject is divided into the following *thirty-one* sections, suitable for a month's daily use:—

Heaven Revealed.	The New Jerusalem.
Heaven Prepared.	Heavenly Knowledge.
The Beatific Vision.	Heavenly Service.
The Perfected Likeness.	Heavenly Satisfaction.
A World of Light.	Heavenly Society.
A World of Life.	Recognition in Heaven.
A World of Love.	A Father's House.
A Place of Rest.	A Home of Children.
A Harbour of Safety.	The Crown of Glory.
An Abode of Peace.	Degrees of Glory.
A Paradise of Joy.	Varieties of Glory.
A Sabbath of Sabbaths.	Progress in Heaven.
A Temple of Praise.	An Eternal Portion.
A Sure Inheritance.	Heaven a Harvest.
The Land of Promise.	Days of Heaven upon
The Celestial City.	Earth.

LONDON: KNIGHT & SON, CLERKENWELL CLOSE.

www.ingramcontent.com/pod-product-compliance
Lightning Source LLC
Chambersburg PA
CBHW030342230426
43664CB00007BA/497